Sheila F. Eismann

# Stirrings of The Spirit

Sheila F. Eismann

# Stirrings of The Spirit

Sheila F. Eismann

Desert Sage Press

## Sheila F. Eismann

Unless otherwise indicated, all Scripture quotations are taken from the New King James Version. Copyright © 1983 by Thomas Nelson, Inc. Used by permission. All rights reserved.

Scripture quotations marked "NIV" are taken from the Holy Bible, New International Version ®, Copyright 1973, 1978, 1984 by International Bible Society. Used by permission of Zondervan Publishing House. All rights reserved.

Copyright © 2013 by Sheila F. Eismann. All rights reserved.
Fifth printing - 2016
Published by Desert Sage Press

Cover photo by Sharon Breshears, Ms. Shutterbug Photography. Used by permission. All rights reserved.
Enhanced graphics by Mike P. Reynolds
Edited by JoEllen Claypool, Ruby Keesee, and Joanna Tucker

Printed and bound in the United States of America. All rights reserved. No part of this publication may be reproduced or transmitted in any form or by any means, electronic, mechanical, or digital including photocopying, recording, or by an information storage and retrieval system – except by a reviewer who may quote brief passages and in a review to be printed in a magazine, newspaper, or by the Web – without written permission from the publisher.

# Stirrings of The Spirit

Any trademarks, service marks, product names or named features are used only for reference and are assumed to be the property of their respective owners, and the use of any one of those terms does not imply an endorsement on the part of the author and the publisher.

ISBN: 978-0615720203
Library of Congress Control Number: 2012953877

To order additional autographed copies of this book, please contact sheila@sheilaeismann.com.
 Books are also available:
www.sheilaeismann.com
www.amazon.com
www.etsy.com/shop/BooksbySheilaEismann

Sheila F. Eismann

# DEDICATION

This literary endeavor is dedicated to the Holy Spirit of God, the Third Person of The Trinity, Who has been my Helper, Paraclete,[1] Comforter, and Teacher since I accepted Jesus Christ as my personal Lord and Savior in August of 1983.

With the assistance of the Holy Spirit, I began penning annual Prophetic Journals commencing in 1988. I will be forever grateful for the information contained therein as I drew heavily upon it while presenting the testimonies in the following pages for your enjoyment and encouragement.

Sheila F. Eismann

# ACKNOWLEDGEMENTS

Words are inadequate to express my sincere thanks and gratitude to my spiritual mentor, friend, and Biblical teacher Ruby Keesee. During the early days of my Christian walk, it was Ruby who took me under her wing and instructed me in the revelatory realms of God, including dreams, visions, and prophetic words. She also encouraged me to write down what I received from the Holy Spirit of God to keep an accurate record thereof. The added benefit to this practice was a building up of my most holy faith [Jude 1:20] as I saw God move powerfully through my life, and the lives of my family members and acquaintances throughout the past three decades.

In addition, I would like to thank JoEllen Claypool and Joanna Tucker who graciously offered their time and assistance with this manuscript.

Lastly, I am grateful for the family members and friends who have walked through so many life experiences with me. I appreciate all of you!

Sheila F. Eismann

# TABLE OF CONTENTS

Dedication ............................................. vii

Acknowledgements ................................ ix

Foreword ............................................... xiii

Introduction .......................................... xvii

Chapter 1 – On the Brink of Disaster .......... 25

Chapter 2 – You Need to Sit This One Out ... 97

Chapter 3 – You're Going Down .................. 105

Chapter 4 – Ya'll Got a Microwave ............. 121

Chapter 5 – The Christmas Surprise ............ 139

Chapter 6 – On That Day The Curtain Was Gray ..................................... 147

Chapter 7 – "Hail, King of the Jews!" .......... 185

Chapter 8 – The Beater with The Heater .... 197

Sheila F. Eismann

**Chapter 9 – From Whence It Came, It Shall Return** ............................................... 211

**Chapter 10 – "Deadly Tornado Rips Across Oklahoma** ........................... 223

Stirrings of The Spirit

## FOREWORD

Reading this most current work of author Sheila Eismann was an incredible experience. Many writings can be enjoyed and are informational, but it is a rare work that will make you more aware of your surroundings.

As I was absorbed by the personal testimonies in her book, I was reminded of Job 33:14,

"For God does speak — now one way, now another — though man may not perceive it." [NIV]

Sheila shares the moments that God speaks to her and how she and her family reacted to those situations. She is very transparent with her readers as she reflects on the weak moments that she had as a mom having to watch her daughter go through a horrific accident. However, even in those moments of anger wherein she was not able to perceive the purpose for this ordeal, Sheila kept her faith. She and her husband never gave up praying.

As the author was faced with another trial,

this time involving her husband, she explains the witness that he was to his doctors and nurses through his faith that God was in control. The doctors were able to acknowledge that what they saw firsthand with regard to his healing and recovery was a miracle and commended him on his good attitude throughout the situation.

This book will be an encouragement to all. It will make you examine your own faith and give you a hunger for a deeper relationship with the One and Only, our Creator. It will help you to understand that when you move on the nudging that you are feeling from the Holy Spirit, lives can be transformed. It becomes the ripple effect; you feel prompted to do something, you act on it which can become an answer to somebody else's prayer. That may lead to giving them the confidence that God is moving and they will in turn proceed to do what God is telling them to do.

After reading *Stirrings of The Spirit*, I am making a conscious effort to be more watchful for opportunities that God is laying before me and to listen more intently to the whispers of the Holy Spirit.

Stirrings of The Spirit

------- JoEllen Claypool, Pastor's Wife, Sand Hollow Baptist Church, Caldwell, Idaho; author of *A Realist's Guide to Being a Pastor's Wife*, Valley Walker Press, New Plymouth, Idaho; Member Idaho Authors' Community, and contributing author to *An Eclectic Collage, Volume 2: Relationships of Life*, Freundship Press, Boise, Idaho.

~~~~~~~~~~~~~~~~~~~~

When God makes a promise, God keeps that promise.

*Stirrings of the Spirit* is author Sheila Eismann's testament that what God has promised will come to pass. Throughout her book, Eismann shares stories of miracles that God has wrought in answer to her prayers. Among the miracles Eismann writes about, is the miracle of a life brought back from the brink of death. In the darkest moment, when her daughter's life is slipping away, Eismann holds steadfast to her faith that if God wills it, He will

## Sheila F. Eismann

save her daughter in spite of a doctor's grim pronouncement that her daughter's death is eminent. In addition to her stories of miracles that defy what is known about the physical laws of the universe, Eismann shares her testimony of communication with God through the Spirit and the visions that are received through spiritual communication that forewarn of things to come. Eismann is firm in her belief that when God makes a promise, even if that promise requires supernatural intervention, it will happen.

-------- Joanna Tucker, former editor, retired journalist, Member Idaho Authors' Community, and contributing author to *An Eclectic Collage, Volume 2: Relationships of Life*, Freundship Press, Boise, Idaho.

# INTRODUCTION

Before you launch into this marvelous set of true stories, it is paramount that you know just exactly which spirit is being written about since the title of the book simply reads, *Stirrings of The Spirit*.

In this writing, I will be referring to and giving honor to the Holy Spirit of God, the Third Person of the Trinity.

"Some people insist that the Holy Spirit is an influence – a power or source of God-given spiritual energy. Others see Him as a ghostlike force, entering or leaving us at will. Others picture Him as a kind of cosmic magician, elusive and vague, who drops mysteriously into our lives to make religious things happen and then leaves just as quickly as He came.

The Bible makes it clear, however, that the

Holy Spirit is a person who lives within every Christian. It also teaches that He is God, the Third Person of the Trinity.

The Scriptures give us five clear evidences that the Holy Spirit is a person, not just a mystic force or strange power.

1. **The Holy Spirit is spoken of as 'He.'** Jesus referred to the Holy Spirit as 'He.' He promised His disciples: 'I will pray the Father, and He will give you another Helper, that He [the Holy Spirit] may abide with you forever' (Jn. 14:16)

2. **The Holy Spirit has intelligence.** He knows the 'deep things of God' and reveals them to us (1 Cor. 2:10-11). Only a person has this kind of intelligence.

3. **The Holy Spirit makes decisions.** He gives gifts to the Lord's people, 'distributing to each one individually as He wills' (1 Cor. 12:11). Only a personal being can make decisions.

4. **The Holy Spirit has emotions.** He feels love (Rom. 15:30) and grief (Eph. 4:30). An influence cannot feel emotions like these.

5. **The Holy Spirit is active.** He does things only a person can do:

    - Speaks (Rev. 2:7)
    - Intercedes (Rom. 8:26)
    - Teaches (Jn. 14:26)
    - Leads (Rom. 8:14)
    - Appoints (Acts 20:28)
    - Empowers (Acts 1:8)

## HE IS GOD

The Holy Spirit is also referred to in the Bible as God. He is the Third Person of the eternal Trinity, one with the Father and with the Son. The following factors show His deity:

1. **The Spirit's name appears as equal with the Father and the Son in the formula for baptism and in some of the New Testament prayers.** (Mt. 28:19; 2 Cor. 13:14)

2. **The apostle Peter said that the Holy Spirit was God.** When Ananias' sin was exposed, Peter told him that he had lied to the Holy Spirit. He went on to say that this lie had not been 'to men but to God' (Acts 5:3-4).

3. **The Holy Spirit is called 'Lord'** (2 Cor. 3:17-18).

4. **The Holy Spirit possesses qualities that belong only to God**: eternality (Heb. 9:14), the ability to be everywhere at the same time (Ps.139:7-10), sovereign power (Lk. 1:35, 37), and the knowledge of 'the things of God' (1 Cor. 2:10-12).

The Bible teaches that the Holy Spirit, Who lives within every Christian, is a person and that He is God.   Admittedly we can't grasp the great mystery of how the Holy Spirit can live within us. But we don't have to understand it. We just have to trust that what the Bible says is true."[2]

## Stirrings of The Spirit

I was recently reminded of the fact that we have not been left here on earth to decorate the church but to demonstrate the power of God in visible, credible and authentic living.

Since decorating is not one of my long suits, my primary purpose for writing this book is to share with you the miraculous powers of God. What a glory to behold! So pour yourself a cup of coffee or tea, head to your favorite reading spot, and join me as we walk through a few valleys en route to some mountain tops.

Let our journey begin . . .

Sheila F. Eismann

Stirrings of The Spirit

∞∞∞∞∞∞∞∞∞∞∞∞∞∞∞∞∞∞∞∞∞∞∞∞∞∞∞∞∞∞∞∞∞

"And in that day you will say:

'Praise the LORD, call upon His name;
Declare His deeds among the peoples,
Make mention that His name is exalted.
Sing to the LORD,
For He has done excellent things;
This *is* known in all the earth.
Cry out and shout, O inhabitant of Zion,
For great is the Holy One of Israel in your midst!' "
[Isaiah 12:4-6]


"Therefore He who supplies the Spirit to you and works miracles among you, *does He do it* by the works of the law, or by the hearing of faith?"   [Galatians 3:5]

∞∞∞∞∞∞∞∞∞∞∞∞∞∞∞∞∞∞∞∞∞∞∞∞∞∞∞∞∞∞∞∞∞

Sheila F. Eismann

# 1

## ON THE BRINK OF DISASTER

"Behold, children *are* a heritage from the LORD, the fruit of the womb *is* a reward. Like arrows in the hand of a warrior, so *are* the children of one's youth. Happy *is* the man who has his quiver full of them; they shall not be ashamed, but shall speak with their enemies in the gate." [Psalm 127:3-5]

The year was 1991. It was the year I would ask God for a miracle the magnitude of which would defy the physical laws of the universe. At the brink of disaster, I would have to put everything in God's hands and trust with every ounce of my being that what I asked of Him would happen as He promised.

King Solomon, one of the wisest and most knowledgeable men who ever lived, reminds us in the above two verses from the book of Psalms of our precious heritage.  Perhaps the king penned these particular words as he contemplated laboring and prospering with the Lord.  He was the father of one son named Rehoboam (1 Kings 11:43) and two daughters, Taphath (1 Kings 4:11) and Basemath (1 Kings 4:15). While this chapter does not deal with Biblically recorded nobility per se, it does chronicle an omnipotent outpouring of God's mercy and grace.

On a gorgeous fall day, amidst the picturesque setting of the rolling hills of the Palouse,[3] God blessed us with our second daughter.  Since my doctor had convinced me beyond a shadow of a doubt that she was going to be a boy, I lobbied heavily to name her Cody. One must remember that these were the days in which having an ultrasound prior to a child's birth was not really in vogue.

Immediately upon her delivery, the doctor exclaimed, "Oh my goodness, it's a girl!" Before departing the hospital, there was still a part of me that wanted to pen Cody as the first name on the birth certificate, but we ultimately settled on Christine.  To honor both grandmothers, we had decided that our first daughter would be given her paternal grandmother's first name for her middle name, and Christine would continue the tradition with my mother's first name.

Daughter number two was a charmer from a very young age and developed hilarious pronunciations of words which endeared her to people across the amber colored landscape. Most of her words ended with "oy." For instance, instead of saying, "door," she would say, "doy." If Christi wanted you to open the door for her she would simply request, "Opit da doy floy!"

When our blonde cutie pie would flash her smile, complete with angled cuspids, bat her snappy grayish eyes, and utter a few syllables, this would prompt women to open their purses and start forking over all sorts of goodies. It's no wonder she was nicknamed "Kitten."

If Christi could be outside racing a horse down the bank of a canal, riding a snowmobile, or making mud pies close to a cement ditch on the family farm, her world could not have been any better. I used to describe her as "being born in overdrive" and earnestly desired to have at least one-tenth of her energy.

Being a relatively compliant child growing up, we had few, if any, problems with this daughter. She was just busy and kept everyone else in the same mode.

After accepting Jesus Christ as my personal

Lord and Savior, I began receiving revelatory messages from God in the form of the word of wisdom, the word of knowledge and discerning of spirits. [1 Corinthians 12: 8, 10]  These are explained in greater detail in the Appendix portion in the back of this book.

In 1988 I received a prophetic word from the Lord concerning Christi.  Now, when I say a prophetic word, I am referring to hearing the audible voice of God through the Holy Spirit similar to the account found in Acts 13:2,

"As they [the prophets and teachers in the church at Antioch] ministered to the Lord and fasted, the Holy Spirit said, 'Now separate to Me Barnabas and Saul for the work to which I have called them.' "

The 1988 word was very brief. The Holy Spirit warned me that Christi would get into trouble and would be on the brink of disaster, but that we were to look to God.  The following three key words were deeply imbedded in my memory: **brink of disaster.**

Our daughter proceeded to be very successful in high school and excelled as an athlete as well as gaining both local and national honors in her business related organizations.  She was a relatively easy teenager to raise in view of the fact that she never broke curfew, got into trouble with the law, and so forth. There were times, however, when we did not fully inquire as to the routes traversed in our old brown three-quarter ton Ford Explorer® hunting pickup since it just seemed to always be parked in the designated area each morning.

So with respect to the fulfillment of the 1988 prophetic word, I wanted to dismiss it for the most part as all I could think of with respect to Christi getting into real trouble was with the law, school authorities and what have you. But as the prophet Isaiah so aptly reminded the Israelites in Chapter 55, verses 8-9,

"For My thoughts *are* not your thoughts, nor *are* your ways My ways," says the LORD. 'For *as* the heavens are higher than the earth, so are My ways higher than your ways, and My thoughts than your thoughts.' "

Suffice it to say, God and I obviously were not on the same page with respect to this whole "brink of disaster" thing. On April 13, 1991, during our church's Women's Retreat at Camp Pinewood in McCall, Idaho, my spiritual mentor and dear Christian friend Ruby had the following dream:

## Sheila F. Eismann

"Sheila E. and I were lying in bed at night just like we are in real life at the retreat in McCall, April 1991. The ladies were in bunks all around us asleep just like they really are.

The bed began to shake just like it had during the night as Sheila was restless.

In my dream, Sheila began to speak out in her sleep. She lay there and began to quote scripture. She said, 'Verse 7: Be not dismayed when you are tossed to and fro . . . Verse 8: I will uphold you with my righteous right hand . . . I will rock you like a baby.'

In my dream I listened carefully so I could write it down afterwards and tell her. **I reached over and turned on a lamp** and wrote it down in my journal, trying to remember all the words.

Sheila awoke (in my dream still) and sat up. I told her about it and she said she had been having a bad dream. I told her, 'No, you were prophesying.'

This was all so real that when I really did wake up I wasn't sure if it had really happened or not. But in real life a lamp **was not** beside my bed. Isaiah 41:10" [End of dream; emphasis mine]

In the context of the above cited verse, God is

Stirrings of The Spirit

assuring Israel of His help wherein He states,

> "Fear not, for I *am* with you;
> Be not dismayed, for I *am* your God.
> I will strengthen you,
> Yes, I will help you,
> I will uphold you with My righteous right hand." [Isaiah 41:10]

Little did I realize at the time how this verse would literally play out over my life within the next year.

Here's a copy of Ruby's dream:

# Sheila F. Eismann

4/13/91 - A dream

Sheila E. and I were lying in bed at night just like we are in real life at the Retreat in McCall, April 91.

The ladies were in bunks all around us asleep just like they really are.

The bed began to shake just like it had during the night as Sheila was restless.

In my dream, Sheila began to speak out in her sleep. She lay there and began to quote scripture (I thought).

She said, "verse 7: Be not dismayed when you are tossed to and fro . . . . . . .

verse 8: I will uphold you with my righteous right hand . . . . . . . . . . . I will rock you like a baby."

In my dream I listened carefully so I could write it down afterwards & tell her. I reached over and turned on a lamp and wrote it down in my journal, trying to remember all the words.

Sheila awoke (in my dream still) and sat up. I told her about it and she said she had been having a bad dream. I told her, "no, you were prophesying."

This was all so real that when I really did awake I wasn't sure if it had really happened or not. But in real life a lamp was not beside my bed. Is 41:10

## Stirrings of The Spirit

How many of you have ever held on so tightly to something or someone that it hurt when God began to pry your fingers loose?

Christi began her senior year of high school in September of 1990, and from that time until her graduation in June of 1991, I began the grieving process for our daughter as she would soon be leaving the nest. I had held on so tightly to our little treasure from heaven that it was excruciatingly painful as God began to require me to turn loose of her.

The exact same day that Christi graduated from high school, she began dating a young man from a nearby town. The courtship continued throughout the summer, and in September he returned to school in California where he was pursuing his master's degree.

The Lord beautifully orchestrated the details to allow our daughter to enroll as a freshman at an outstanding college. You see, He knew that she could not attend a school very far from home. Otherwise, we would have had to take out a second mortgage on our house the first month just to pay the telephone bill! Can any of you relate?

With Christi off to college my nervous system began to calm down somewhat, but the peace within my heart was short-lived.

In October of 1991 our daughter began

planning a trip to sunny California to see her boyfriend over Veteran's Day weekend. Since she did not have a car on campus, the hunt began in earnest for a possible ride to Cali. She found a ride, but then it was cancelled, and I said, "Thank you Lord!"

Are you familiar with the term "strong-willed child"? Just a few short pages ago, I informed you that our daughter was a relatively easy child to raise. Well, that was until she entered college! It was obvious from my talking to Christi that she was going to make the trip over the holiday weekend even if she had to hitch-hike. It was California or bust!

About the third week of October the Holy Spirit began to impress upon me, "The 8th, the 8th, the 8th!" It just kept coming to me in droves. For some reason, all I could think of was January 8th of 1992. I asked my husband what day of the week this date would fall on. He looked ahead to the dates on a checkbook calendar and said that it would be a Wednesday. I did not stop and pray to ask the Lord to show me what was so significant about the 8th.

Also, about this same time, Christi had found a definite ride to San Jose. I still did not have a good feeling about the trip.

On October 30th, 1991, I was downstairs

## Stirrings of The Spirit

getting a birthday card ready for my youngest sister, and I happened to also see two sympathy cards. The Holy Spirit said, "Set those two cards out where you can easily find them. You are going to need them." I could not readily imagine what I would need them for, but I placed them in a visible spot.

The master plan for the California trip was finalized. Christi and two other girls would be leaving the morning of November 8, 1991, at 3:30 a.m. and driving to Sacramento that day.

On the evening of November 7th, I was in the downstairs of our home getting ready to sew a lap quilt that was intended to be Christi's boyfriend's Christmas present. I was having all sorts of problems with my sewing machine. It simply would not sew a single stitch!

After fighting the machine for about two hours, I discovered the reason that it would not perform was because I had the needle in backwards! I had sewn for over twenty years, and that had never happened before. God did not want me sewing. He wanted me praying.

At exactly half past three the morning of November 8th, the Lord awakened me from a deep sleep. I sat bolt upright in my bed. After placing my feet on the bedroom floor, I began weaving beside my bed just like a person spinning out of control.

I wobbled around the end of my bed, went to the bathroom, came back out, promptly crawled back into bed, and fell back asleep. I know that God was trying to wake me up to pray for the girls and their trip as that is the exact time they left the college campus.

That was twice now that the Lord had called me to pray. I was not very obedient, was I?

Later that morning, I went back downstairs to sew on the lap quilt. At that time, we had only one house phone which was mounted on the upstairs kitchen wall. It had a 40-foot cord that could be stretched into the adjoining laundry room so Christi could sit on the washer and dryer and yak on the phone all hours of the day or night.

At 11:00 a.m. the telephone rang several times and I asked our young son to answer it. Since he was busy playing with his toys, he did not want to and told me as much. We had no answering machine connected to our phone system.

I finally made it back upstairs and answered the telephone. A female voice on the other end asked for my husband, and I told her that he was not home and could I please take a message for him. At this point, my mind was at least 1,000 miles away.

I thought the woman on the telephone was

some sort of sales person trying to sell us something. She asked who I was and how I was related to my husband. In my mind nothing of any importance was clicking. I was thinking, "I wish this gal would just give me the sales pitch for the magazines she is peddling or whatever and hang up the telephone."

Then the woman asked, "Do you have a daughter named Christine?" to which I replied, "Yes." At this point, she identified herself as the nurse from the local trauma center.

The conversation continued with, "Now I want you to remain calm when I tell you this . . . "And then I knew.

Her voice resumed, "Christine has been involved in a car accident and has been flown to our trauma center here at the hospital." I was beyond stunned!

I began to shake all over, and it was all I could do to remain standing. I grabbed hold of the kitchen counter for extra support. The trauma nurse told me to stay at our house and not attempt to drive anywhere. Someone would be sent from the college to get me.

Fortunately my husband Dan just happened to be close to the trauma center attending a meeting, so I contacted him and told him what had happened. I asked him to go to the hospital immediately and call me as soon as he found out the details. I waited inside our home for one hour before he returned my call, and that had to be the longest hour of my entire life. Our young son and I just cried and prayed as I held him in my lap in the rocking chair in our living room. We lived in a small rural town one hour and 15 minutes from the hospital.

When my husband called back, he informed me that Christi had been ejected from the back seat of the vehicle, and had sustained head and back injuries. With a quivering and barely audible voice he said, "Sheila, she is in very critical condition."

A short while later, a kindhearted woman from the college drove into our driveway to pick up our son and me to take us to the hospital. When I stepped outside our front door to go with her, I discovered that she was driving the same type of vehicle in which my daughter was riding when the accident occurred. I exclaimed, "Lord, are You trying to test my sense of humor or what? First, my daughter crashes in one of these, and now You want me to ride to the hospital in one!"

When I arrived at the trauma center, Christi was still tied down to the bed and was fading in and out of consciousness. From outward appearances, it did not look like she was hurt very badly. Her hands were all chewed up with gravel inside them.

Christi would cry out, "Untie me, please," to which I would reply, "Honey, I can't untie you," and then she would start to cry. She would lay there as if asleep, and then suddenly attempt to sit up, while shouting nonsensical things, such as: "Turn the page! Turn the page!", or "Grab the box! The papers are flying away!"

I just stood by the side of her bed and prayed. At precisely 3:00 p.m. the Holy Spirit spoke to my heart the comforting words from Jeremiah 20:11a [NIV],

"But the LORD is with me like a mighty warrior;"

At half past five in the afternoon the doctors moved Christi from the trauma center to the sixth floor critical care unit, and it was nine o'clock that night before we could even get inside her room to see her.

With the accident happening out of state, the details remained fairly sketchy at this point. Basically what happened was that the three students had left the campus at 3:30 a.m. on Friday morning, November 8, 1991. After stopping at a local station to gas up the car, Christi made herself a little bed in the back of the vehicle and proceeded to fall fast asleep.

They traveled in a dense fog for approximately 150 miles before the driver of the vehicle fell asleep. It was approximately 5:30 a.m. when the car drifted off the right side of the road, striking a metal reflector. That apparently awakened the driver who over-corrected, flipping the vehicle.

After rolling several times, the car ended up on its wheels off the highway. On the first roll, the front left corner of the roof caved in, killing the driver instantly. The front seat passenger had been wearing a seat belt, and was uninjured except for minor bumps and scratches. When the car stopped rolling, the passenger looked at the driver and knew immediately that she was dead. She got out of the vehicle and began to stumble through the darkness toward the highway. En route, she tripped over Christi. God in His providence kept the passenger in the front seat alive to go for help. He also kept her from instantly going into shock so she could summon help. Shortly after this occurred, two hunters came by, and you guessed it, in the same type of vehicle as was involved in the accident and the same type as the one that had transported our young son and me to the trauma center.

One of the hunters had first aid training and

## Stirrings of The Spirit

knew enough to cover Christi and not to move her. The hunters also had a CB radio and somehow (the range of a CB radio is much too short for them to have contacted the ambulance directly) they started a wave of CB messaging. The hunter radioed a trucker who passed the message on to another trucker up the road who did the same until one was close enough to contact the closest ambulance crew. Shortly after leaving the city limits, the ambulance driver radioed the trauma center's rescue helicopter because it was too slow driving in the dense fog.

The helicopter pilot was stirred in his spirit to report to work early on that particular Friday morning and arrived just before the call came in. There just happened to be all male nurses working the shift.

The pilot and his crew took off immediately at about 8:55 a.m. to begin the 120-mile trip to the accident scene. During the flight there, he was unable to see the ground because of the pea-soup like fog. He had flown the area enough, however, to know approximately where the accident scene was located. He also knew that if the fog covered the area, as it normally did, the accident scene would be shrouded in fog, making it unsafe to land. In fact, he and the crew discussed turning back.

41

He said that had it been a female crew that morning, they probably would have turned back. The male crew was more foolhardy, however, and decided to press on. Thank God!

Fortunately, mounted within this particular air ambulance was a computer that took its signals from a satellite which enabled it to land within 50 feet of an accident scene. The pilot had to fight a strong head-wind that morning because the wind was blowing opposite its usual direction for that time of year. As he approached the accident scene, the pilot realized that the wind was blowing the fog AWAY from the accident scene. The edge of the fog bank ended approximately one mile from where the accident had occurred. If it weren't for the unusual wind direction, they would have been unable to land.

My husband, who completed two tours of duty in Vietnam as a door gunner on a UH1B Huey Helicopter, commented afterwards that after flying that many missions, he was well aware that they could not have landed safely in dense fog. I believe the Lord stirred up the wind to clear the accident scene.

The air ambulance arrived just as the ground ambulance crew was loading Christi. They transferred her to the helicopter and it headed for the trauma center.

Stirrings of The Spirit

This particular air ambulance could only take one passenger at a time. If there had been two people who were critically injured, the crew would have taken the most critically injured person and let the ground ambulance crew take the other one. All of the equipment that was present in the trauma center was also aboard the air ambulance.

With the accident occurring at approximately five-thirty in the morning and Christi arriving at the trauma center at 10:30 a.m., God had clearly sent His ministering angels to watch over her and keep her alive those five hours in the desert. The first hour after an accident is the most critical, and she had lain in the cold black desert for three hours alone before the air ambulance could get there. That first hour following an accident is referred to by medical personnel as **The Golden Hour.**[4] Hebrews 1:14 speaks of angels being ministering spirits sent forth to minister to those who will inherit salvation.

At 9:30 p.m. on the evening of the accident, a group of us met in the fourth floor chapel of the hospital for prayer, and the Holy Spirit brought to my remem-brance Psalm 50:14-15 which reads:

## Sheila F. Eismann

"Offer to God thanksgiving,
And pay your vows to the Most High.
Call upon Me in the day of trouble;
I will deliver you, and you shall glorify Me."

At 12:30 a.m. on the morning of November 9th, I was lying in bed praying, and the Holy Spirit spoke to my heart and said, "The Lord of the Sabbath can heal on the Sabbath." The premise of this is taken from Matthew 12:1-13 which reads as follows:

"At that time Jesus went through the grain fields on the Sabbath. And His disciples were hungry, and began to pluck heads of grain and to eat. And when the Pharisees saw *it*, they said to Him, 'Look, Your disciples are doing what is not lawful to do on the Sabbath!' But He said to them, 'Have you not read what David did when he was hungry, he and those who were with him: how he entered the house of God and ate the showbread which was not lawful for him to eat, nor for those who were with him, but only for the priests? Or have you not read in the law that on the Sabbath the priests in the temple profane the Sabbath, and are blameless? Yet I say to you that in this place there is *One* greater than the temple. But if you had known what *this* means, *'I desire mercy and not sacrifice,'* you would not have condemned the guiltless. For the Son of Man is Lord even of the Sabbath.' Now when He had departed from there, He went into their synagogue. And behold, there was a man who had a withered hand. And they asked Him, saying, 'Is it lawful to heal on the Sabbath?'—that they might accuse Him. Then He said to them, 'What man is there among you who has one sheep, and if it falls into a pit on the Sabbath, will not lay hold of it and lift *it* out? Of how much more value then is a man than a sheep? Therefore it is lawful to do good on the Sabbath.' Then He said to the man, 'Stretch out your hand.' And he stretched *it* out, and it was restored as whole as the other.' "

In those early morning hours, I asked God for two things:

(1) The Holy Spirit gift of healing (1 Corinthians 12:9) for Christi; and
(2) The Holy Spirit gift of faith (1 Corinthians 12:9) for me.

Suffice it to say, Christi was in no shape to exercise her own faith or ask for healing. Now readers, this had been one **LONG** day!

For the next couple of days there was no change in Christi's general condition which was as follows:

- She was unconscious.
- Her lungs were bruised.
- She suffered five compression fractures in her back.
- There were bruises to the frontal lobes of her brain (subdural hematoma).
- There was bleeding inside her brain.
- Her brain was swelling. Because the skull prevents the brain from expanding outward, it fills the available space within the skull, constricting blood vessels. If the swelling becomes too severe, the blood flow is cut off, and the brain dies. In general, the brain continues to swell for 3-5 days after a traumatic accident similar to the one heretofore mentioned.
- Her left ear drum was torn.
- Christi was hooked up to a respirator because she could not breathe on her own.
- There were two aspects of the brain injury which were important at this point. Because Christi was asleep when the accident occurred, the net effect was

that the force of impact was greater. When someone hits the back of his or her head, it naturally shoves the brain forward and slams it into the front of the skull.

Her neurosurgeon used several techniques to try to keep the swelling in Christi's brain at a minimum. He kept her as dehydrated as possible. To facilitate this, he drilled a hole through her skull into one of the ventricles in her brain, into which he placed a tube which served two functions.

First, it was attached to a device to measure the pressure within her skull (the intracranial pressure, also known as ICP). A normal ICP is 15. When Christi's ICP increased to 20, it would trigger an alarm. The nurse on duty could then try to relieve the pressure by opening a little tap attached to the tube and draining a few drops of the cerebral fluid from the ventricle.

If draining the fluid did not lower the pressure, or there was none to drain, they would then increase Christi's respiration rate to hyper-oxygenate her blood (she was intubated – had a tube down her throat to pump air into her lungs). If that did not work, then the hospital personnel gave her two drugs. The first would cause fluid to go from her brain to the rest of her body and the second, given about 20 minutes later, would cause her kidneys to extract fluid from her body and excrete it into her urine.

**November 10th, 1991 – 2 days later:**

At 6:30 a.m. God spoke to my heart and said, "I will heal her."

This same day, which was a Sunday, we spoke with Christi's neurosurgeon who informed us that we still had a couple of white knuckle days left. What he was really saying was that we still needed to wait 2-3 days to see if the brain would stop swelling and we would still have a daughter who was alive.

**November 11th, 1991 – 3 days later:**

At 12:30 p.m. on Monday our pastor, my husband, and I gathered at Christi's bedside to pray for her. When I laid my hands on our daughter to pray, I heard the Holy Spirit say, "Take up your mat and walk." These are the same words that Jesus spoke to the paralytic in Capernaum in the second chapter of the gospel of Mark, verses 1-12 (NIV).

Stirrings of The Spirit

On November 12th I prayed and asked God for the Holy Spirit's gift of miracles for Christi. (1 Corinthians 12:10).

When Christi's medical team could see that she had survived for five days following her accident, they fitted her with an orthopedic jacket, also known as "a clam shell," to support her back and compression fractures.

**November 13th, 1991 – five days later and our wedding anniversary:**

As the nurse was suctioning Christi, she told her to open her eyes and she did for about 30 seconds! The nurse said, "Squeeze my hand," and Christi did.

I leaned over the side of her bed and said, "Christi, this is Mom. I love you. Can you open your eyes?" She held her eyes open for about 10 seconds. I continued with, "If you can hear me, squeeze my hand," and she responded accordingly. That was the best anniversary gift I could have received.

I prayed and asked God to surround Christi's bed with healing angels. Through the Holy Spirit's gift of discerning of spirits, He showed me a vision in which He had placed five angels around her bedside.[5] These angels were different than others that I had previously seen during my revelatory encounters with the Lord.

These particular angels resembled scholarly men with shoulder length dark hair. Each of them was clothed in a white robe. One angel was assigned specifically to her head and touched it periodically. The remaining angels touched the vertebrae in her back. Please refer to the Appendix at the back of this book for further explanation of the Holy Spirit gift of discerning of spirits. [1 Corinthians 12:10]

**November 16th, 1991 – 8 days later:**

Again, I heard the voice of God very early in the day, "I will raise her up on the last day."

At 5:00 p.m. Christi awakened for about two minutes and waved at me! I was ecstatic! She appeared confused, did not know anyone, but did know that she was in the hospital. From the fifth day through the eighth day she would open her eyes occasionally, usually when the medical personnel would suction her, but she remained unconscious the entire time.

**November 17th, 1991 – 9 days later – Sunday morning:**

## Stirrings of The Spirit

My husband, son, and I arrived at the hospital around 10:00 a.m. Per our usual procedure, my husband first called back to Christi's critical care nurse to request permission to see our daughter. The nurse told him to wait 20 minutes and then call again. We were not immediately concerned because the medical personnel routinely had to do things to her that they thought would upset us if we watched. As we became better acquainted with the nurses and respiratory therapists, they would allow us to stay in the room while performing those procedures. We just thought that the personnel on duty this particular morning might be people we did not know or had not previously met. We were also informed that the neurosurgeon, to whom Christi had originally been assigned when she arrived at the hospital on November 8th, was out of town for the weekend and one of his fellow doctors was filling in for him.

Dan called back to the nurses' station 20 minutes later. This time, the nurse on duty told him to wait 20 more minutes and then just head back to Christi's hospital room. After waiting again, we finally headed back and were met in the hallway by her physical therapist who informed us that we could not see our daughter right then because they were going to do a CAT

Scan (Computerized Axial Tomography Scan) which would take about an hour and then we would be able to see her. We returned to the waiting room.

Next, we saw them wheel Christi down the hall en route to the radiology department, and about an hour later we saw them wheel her back toward her room. Then we headed for her room so we could see her. This time we were met by a nurse who told us that they were putting Christi into a barbiturate coma. According to this nurse, Christi's ICP had risen because she had become too hydrated the last several days. They were going to put her into this coma and dehydrate her. The nurse further stated that this procedure was nothing serious and that it would merely set our daughter's recovery back several days.

My husband knew, however, that the barbiturate coma was not merely a routine procedure. While chatting with a nurse during Christi's first day in ICU, she had told him that although our daughter's condition was very serious, it could be worse. Her exact words had been, "At least they have not put her into a barbiturate coma." That was the treatment of final resort – a last ditch effort to save a patient's life. The barbiturate coma basically

## Stirrings of The Spirit

shuts down as much of the bodily functions as possible to try to buy some extra time.

Dan and I returned to the waiting room. At this point, we were not overly concerned that Christi was in imminent danger, primarily because the nurse had assured us that this was merely a minor setback. We were, however, deeply saddened that her recovery would be delayed and her suffering prolonged. It was difficult to stand beside Christi's hospital bed and feel so helpless.

At 2:30 p.m. we received a page from the neurosurgeon to go back to our daughter's room. When we arrived at the nurses' station outside Christi's hospital room, we found the doctor sitting on a secretarial type chair and rolling back and forth on a plastic mat located by the nurses' station. He was extremely distraught, flailing his arms in the air and running his hands through his hair.

When Dan peered into Christi's room, he saw four people hovering over her, working feverishly. The doctor tried to remain steady as he informed us that despite having done everything he could, "We're probably going to lose her." He had consulted with another neurosurgeon as to her present condition and they had collectively determined that surgery would not help at this point.

He looked me straight in the eye and said, "This is scary business."

I replied, "**I KNOW** this is scary business. That's my baby that's lying in that bed!"

By this time, Christi's intracranial pressures were in the 60's and climbing. (Remember, normal is 15 and below). I asked the doctor if there was one large clot in her brain to which he replied, "No, there are several small blood clots." He ended by saying, "Her condition is compatible with life, but I don't think she is going to make it."

My husband asked the doctor if we could go in and lay hands on Christi and offer prayer for her. After consulting with the nurses, he calmly replied, "Sure, you might as well. That's about all you've got left now." Dan and I then went into her room, laid hands on her, and prayed.

After praying over our treasure from heaven, I walked out of Christi's room and down the corridor of the ICU floor to the waiting room screaming at the top of my lungs, "God, I'm not ready to give her up yet! It wasn't supposed to happen like this."

But, it never is supposed to happen like this, is it?

The next couple of hours seemed like I was not even on planet earth. I can remember my dear friend Charleen coming to the hospital. After she found out the prognosis, she jumped into action and started calling various prayer chains to place our daughter on them. This in turn activated other prayer chains, and there were people praying in Vietnam, Scotland and all across the globe.

About 6:00 p.m. my oldest brother, a practicing physician at the time, called my husband on the telephone located outside the waiting room. Prior to calling Dan, my brother had contacted the nursing station to get Christi's diagnosis. He informed my husband that our daughter had venous sinus thrombosis. The venous sinuses drain venous blood from your brain into your jugular veins. "Venous sinus thrombosis" meant that Christi had blood clots in her venous sinuses.

My brother continued with the fact that there were gram negative rods in Christi's cerebral fluid. Gram negative rods are bacteria found in your intestines. Somehow, those bacteria had gotten into her brain, causing a severe infection.

We were also informed that the organ donor team wanted to speak with us to obtain consent to donate Christi's organs, but they were afraid to approach us.

Sheila F. Eismann

At this point we asked to speak to the neurosurgeon, but he refused to see us. When we returned to our daughter's hospital room, it was obvious that the medical personnel on the ICU floor had given up on her. Her clam shell brace had now been removed and was lying in the corner of her room. The rules governing our visits with her also changed. Before, we had to call back to the nurses' station to obtain permission to visit; she could have visitors for only 5 minutes every hour with only two visitors at a time; and we were not to make any loud noises (a comatose person can still hear, and loud noises stimulate brain activity, which in turn would cause her ICP to rise). Now, we were told that those rules no longer applied. We could come back any time and stay as long as we wanted, and there were no restrictions on the number of people who could be in her room at one time. Another sign that the ICU staff had given up on Christi was that they would no longer look at us when we were walking back to her room. They would turn their heads, obviously not wanting to make eye contact. I cannot even imagine how hard it must be on a daily basis for these merciful people to watch people die.

In our hearts we knew that all of the medical personnel had done everything within their earthly power to save our daughter's life. They had gone above and beyond the call of duty in every aspect, which we definitely appreciated.

We spent the next several hours between Christi's room and the chapel praying with our Christian friends. At one point, while we were in her room, my husband told her respiratory therapist that sometimes God lets us get to the very end of our rope before He intervenes. The therapist responded, "We're there!"

By this time, word had gone out all across our valley that we were going to lose our daughter. People began to come to the sixth floor of the hospital in droves. There literally was no place to sit or stand in the waiting room or as far as the eye could see down the hall corridor. People were packed in there like sardines in a can.

A short while later, one of our dear Christian brothers named Al came over and knelt down beside me. He placed his hand on my shoulder and said, "Sheila, you know that if there was anything in the world that I could do to bring Christi back I would do it." His sentiment was probably the norm for most everyone there. This really ministered to me in a fatherly sort of way as my dad was out of town when all of this happened and had not yet returned so he could visit us in the hospital.

As the clock in the waiting room struck 8:00 p.m., the medical staff asked us to have our friends and family leave because there were too many inside and outside the waiting room. At our request, our friends and family then left.

At about 9:00 p.m. a hospital chaplain came back into Christi's room. He said that there was nothing more they could do and that we should go home and get some sleep. He then added, "You can come back in the morning and tell us what you want done with her body." To me, the chaplain's words were more ominous than the neurosurgeon's words earlier that day. Earlier, the neurosurgeon had said he did not think Christi would live. Now, according to the chaplain, the neurosurgeon was sure she would die.

The substitute neurosurgeon's plan was to keep our daughter in the barbiturate coma until Monday morning when the originally assigned neurosurgeon could deal with the situation, in the unlikely event she was still alive. We were told to go home that night and come back the next morning and advise the hospital personnel which morgue we had selected so Christi's body could be delivered there.

Stirrings of The Spirit

We paid one more visit to Christi's room before driving back home late that night. She was no longer hooked up to the breathing tube, and the once energetic, life-filled, beautiful athletic girl was now lying motionless. Her hands were all withered and turning blue as was her face, and her partially opened eyes were rolled back in her head. There was such a presence of death I could no longer stand to be in her hospital room. I was beyond overwhelmed and devastated.

Dan and I drove home late that night, and as we were descending down the steep hill en route to our house, he asked me if we had any life insurance policies on our children. I could not have even told you my own name at that point much less anything about a life insurance policy. When we arrived home, I did in fact go downstairs and look around for awhile and finally found the paperwork. I walked back up the stairs and placed it on the kitchen table.

As I lay in bed that night, I wrestled with God for several hours. I thought of the Biblical account wherein Jacob wrestled with God (Genesis 32:22-32).

I cried out to God ~~

- You spoke and the universe was created

- You parted the Red Sea
- You raised Lazarus and Jesus from the dead
- You can raise Christi from the dead!

I continued with, "God, I don't get it. You spoke to my heart through Your Holy Spirit and said:

- That the Lord of the Sabbath can heal on the Sabbath;
- That You would heal Christi;
- That she would take up her mat and walk;
- You surrounded her hospital bed with healing angels; and
- That You would raise her up on the last day and God, this is the LAST day!"

So, back to the original word that I received from the Holy Spirit in 1988, we literally were *On the Brink of Disaster*...

I could relate to Abraham in the Old Testament when God requested that he offer Isaac unto Him. (Genesis 22:1-14). I envisioned myself in the throne room of heaven with an altar in front of me. In a spiritual act conducted in my mind, I laid Christi on the altar and said, "God, she's Yours."

Then I began the infamous bartering system with God. My terms were, "If You will keep her alive and heal her, then I'll do anything in Your kingdom that you ask me to do." Aren't we humans interesting at times? I thank God for His patience and longsuffering. Let's see, it's only twenty one years later that I am writing this book . . .

There were many all night prayer vigils conducted on Christi's behalf. Her fellow college students bombarded the throne room of heaven pleading with God to spare Christi's life as the fragrant incense of the saints was being poured out in many geographic areas. (Rev. 5:8; 8:3-4).

God stretched me to total faith and surrender. The words of the Apostle Paul from 2 Corinthians 1:8-11 flashed through my spirit:

> "For we do not want you to be ignorant, brethren, of our trouble which came to us in Asia: that we were burdened beyond measure, above strength, so that we despaired even of life. Yes, we had the sentence of death in ourselves, that we should not trust in ourselves but in God who raises the dead, who delivered us from

so great a death, and does deliver us; in whom we trust that He will still deliver *us*, you also helping together in prayer for us, that thanks may be given by many persons on our behalf for the gift *granted* to us through many."

**November 18th – 10 days later:**

When we arrived at the hospital on Monday morning, lo and behold, Christi was still alive! Her ICP's were back down in the 20's. The doctors, nurses and various hospital personnel kept coming into her room and offering their condolences as they had heard that she was going to die.

Finally, at about 10:00 that morning we met with the neurosurgeon who had been assigned to our daughter when she had first been brought into the trauma center. He had been out of town for 3 days, and the fill-in neurosurgeon had been assigned to care for Christi. Neuro #1, as I referred to him in later years, informed us, "that he was not willing to throw in the towel, and he was going to try to put the pieces of the puzzle back together." For you see, everything that had happened up to this point in time became a supreme mental challenge for this care provider. He indicated that he had indeed reviewed all of the medical records thus far, but he wanted to confirm for himself what had occurred.

The doctor informed us that for Christi to have gotten so bad so quickly, it had to be a problem with a blood vessel in her brain. The first thing he wanted to do was an MRI to see if there were clots in her veins. Dan asked him what would be the chance that the blood clots were gone. He responded, "Not one in a hundred," but his tone of voice and demeanor indicated that he did not think the odds were even that good.

Christi's doctor proceeded to order an MRI to see if there were still blood clots present in her brain. The MRI machine he wanted to use was a portable unit which was parked outside in the hospital parking lot. This contributed to the ongoing precariousness of the procedure as the hospital staff had to wheel her outside in the rain into the mobile unit. We stood inside her hospital room and watched outside the window as the drama unfolded.

The MRI machine uses strong magnets and so metallic equipment cannot be used near it. Because the hospital did not have a nonmetallic ventilator, the staff had to fashion a twenty-foot hose from tracheotomy tubes in order to pump air by hand into Christi's lungs during the procedure. They also had to make long tubing for her intravenous dopamine drop to maintain her blood pressure.

The MRI results showed no clots. There were only iron deposits where the original blood clots had been. God had supernaturally dissolved the clots in her brain, so He had in fact begun the healing process on our Sabbath Day – quite late in the day, but on the Sabbath Day, nonetheless!

The doctor then completed a sonogram to check the arteries in Christi's brain. That test also showed no blockage. The neurosurgeon resolved, "We're going for broke! We are going to pull her out of the barbiturate coma." The medical personnel could not assess her brain function while she was being given barbiturates. They stopped giving her the barbiturates that Monday afternoon, but there was still a risk as her ICP's could shoot way up once again or she could be brain dead. It remained a severe gamble.

**November 20th– 12 days later:**

En route to the hospital that day, I dropped off my husband's work shirts as the students on the college campus had offered to iron them, provide child care for our young son, or perform whatever tasks we needed done.

Upon arriving in Christi's room, we received our first positive sign! When the nurse shone a flashlight into her eyes, her pupils constricted which indicated that her brain stem was still functioning.

As I was standing around the side of her bed, I received another heavenly vision wherein I saw God move five more healing angels around Christi's hospital bed making a total of ten angels. She was battling a high white blood cell count and fever which meant infection was starting to set into her body. The doctor originally assigned to her drilled a new hole in the top of her head so that the swelling would start to go down and her brain ventricles would begin to open up.

Right before I left the hospital that evening, I saw in the Spirit where God had planted a large warrior angel just inside Christi's hospital room. This particular angel maintained a very serious countenance and constantly kept a drawn sword at its side.

### November 21st – 13 days later:

God spoke to my heart and reminded me to forgive any of the medical personnel against whom I might be harboring any type of ill will. How many of you know that sin breaks communion with God?  As Israel's King David stated in verses 18-19 of the 66th Psalm in the NIV, "If I had cherished sin in my heart, the Lord would not have listened; but God has surely listened and heard my voice in prayer."

There are other scriptures that address this heart attitude as well. For you see, Christi's situation had to get that dire before God performed His miracle.  The purpose of a miracle is to glorify God.  This is illustrated in the account following the tenth plague on all of the firstborn in Egypt as the Israelites were preparing to cross the Red Sea on dry ground.

> "Then the LORD said to Moses, 'Why are you crying out to me?  Tell the Israelites to move on.  Raise your staff and stretch out your hand over the sea to divide the water so that the Israelites can go through the sea on dry ground.  I will harden the hearts of the Egyptians so that they will go in after them.  And I will gain glory through Pharaoh and all his army, through his chariots and his horsemen. The Egyptians will know that I am the LORD when I gain

glory through Pharaoh, his chariots and his horsemen.' "[Exodus 14:15-18 NIV]

**November 22nd – 14 days later:**

This is the day Christi awakened!  I just knew that she would wake up, as this was the first day that I had decided to stay home from the hospital, as I was growing so weary.  Dan called me from the hospital to tell me the good news.  I ran out of the house as fast as I could, climbed in our car and drove the hour and fifteen minutes to the hospital.  Later in the day I realized it was the 14th day after the accident, and fourteen is the number in Biblical symbolism for deliverance or salvation.[6]

When she first awakened, our daughter was very angry and then transitioned into the agitated stage.  She jerked out her feeding tube, her catheter, the stitches in her head, and her tracheotomy tube, and she tried to peel her clam shell off, etc. Suffice it to say, she was one busy patient!

The nurses had to tie her ankles and wrists to the bed rails to keep her from pulling the tubes out with her hands and toes.  She would not respond to us at all, other than glaring in anger, so we did not know whether she even knew who we were or could understand what we were saying.

During the second day she was awake, the Lord gave Dan an idea. He took our son into Christi's room and told her that Matt wanted to squeeze her hand. She looked over at her brother, and then extended her hand the best she could with her wrist tied to the rail. It was at that point we realized that she knew us and could understand what we were asking her to do.

## November 24th – 16 days later:

Sunday afternoon I was entering my daily notes into the spiral bound theme notebook that I carried in my purse, when I heard footsteps coming down the hallway. Within a few seconds we were greeted by none other than Tom, the Associate Pastor of our church, and his wife Linda who drove over to see us after weekly services that day.

Tom, all decked out in his brown leather jacket and matching cowboy boots, looked like the cat that swallowed the canary, minus the feathers sticking out of his mouth. Linda's countenance reflected that she was a member of the Joy-bell Committee as well. During Tom's early morning Bible reading that day, The Holy

## Stirrings of The Spirit

Spirit had reminded him of the passage of scripture in Genesis 50:19-20:

> "Joseph said to them [his brothers], 'Do not be afraid, for *am* I in the place of God? But as for you, you meant evil against me; *but* God meant it for good, in order to bring it about as *it is* this day, to save many people alive.' "

In these verses, Joseph was instructing his brothers not to fear him, but to fear God; to humble themselves before God, and to seek His forgiveness.

At the conclusion of his prayer time that morning, Tom sensed that he and Linda were to drive to the hospital after church services and pay us a visit as we could sure use a word of encouragement. He further explained that even though evil may have been intended by the enemy of our souls, God was going to turn it for good and for His glory.

I felt the slap-anointing coming upon me right after this to help keep my flesh in check. There was part of me that wanted to say, "Tom, how can you just waltz in here today with your beautiful blonde wife and act like you don't have a care in the world? Do you even have a clue as to what we have lived through the past sixteen days?"

Yes, trauma and stress do these sorts of things to us. We can experience a myriad of emotions in a New York Minute.[7] After I cooled my jets a bit, I thanked Tom and Linda profusely for delivering that word and praying for us. This couple has a heart as big as all outdoors and would literally do anything they could to help out in similar situations. I still remember that hospital visit to this day. God knew I needed to hear what His servant had to say. In a strange sort of way, it helped to put some things into perspective for me, if that was possible.

### November 25th– 17 days later:

Christi finally recognized me and knew who I was. What a relief! In Biblical symbolism, the number 17 symbolizes victory.[8]

The twentieth day following the accident was Thanksgiving, so my husband, son, and I went to the hospital to spend the day with Christi. Hospital cafeteria food never tasted so good! In the afternoon, she was moved to the sixth floor in the west part of the hospital wing designed for less critical patients. I told her that day God was in the process of healing her, but it was going to take time. I also told her that we had been praying for her. Christi's sister had called to wish the family a Happy Thanksgiving and wanted to remind Christi that she loved her. When I asked her if she remembered her sister she said, "Yes," and when I asked her if she remembered our dear Christian friend Charleen, she replied, "No."

Christi required a very watchful eye around the clock. She had blue colored ropes to keep her tied down very closely to the bed so she could not continue to remove her feeding tube and interfere with the necessary medical instruments. At times, it was like going 15 rounds with a heavy weight boxer to keep her lying flat on the bed and to prevent her from untying the ropes.

We worked out a system to have someone with her 24 hours a day. I would leave our house at about 6:45 every morning with Matt, drop him off at a local day care or a friend's house, and arrive after 8:00 a.m., to be with Christi all day. When Dan got off work at 5:00 p.m., he would pick Matt up from either the day care or a friend's house and drive to the hospital. I would then drive back home with Matt, and Dan would be with Christi until about 10:00 p.m., when other family members and close friends would be with her until I arrived the next morning. We were beyond grateful for those who willingly gave up their valuable sleeping time to help with our daughter.

On the 24th day Christi started going through drug withdrawal effects as the medical personnel determined it was time to wean her from all of the necessary pharmaceuticals that she had been given. Once again, God gave me a vision wherein I saw that He had moved five small warrior angels in above her head and they just constantly flew around in a circle. There was a whirring noise emitted in the spirit realm as the angels continued in their circular routine. The warrior angels had been assigned to battle the effects of drug withdrawal. One of the key factors, however, in her healing would be that she had been drug-and-alcohol free prior to her accident.

### December 6th - 28 days later:

This is the first day that Christi actually remembered anything and realized that she had been in an auto accident. She was moved to the rehabilitation unit on the second floor of the hospital. After lengthy medical evaluations, it was determined that she had awakened at the equivalent of a first-grade student.

Christi required very extensive speech, physical, and occupational therapy. She had to learn how to walk again. The first few sessions in this area were quite discouraging. The physical therapist would place a blue belt approximately ten inches wide around Christi's waist. The belt had ropes attached to it which was guided along by the therapist. When Christi first tried to walk, she would move one foot very slowly, try to steady herself, and then take another step. It took her about twelve minutes to take just a few steps. This whole exercise really pulled my heart strings and I would silently call upon the name of the Lord to help her as she was trying to walk.

Since both of Christi's vocal cords were paralyzed, it was a real project to try to get her to swallow anything. She also required someone sitting at her bedside at all times to monitor her behavior. It was estimated that she would be handicapped for over one year and that it would also be at least that length of time before she could operate a motor vehicle again.

During her third visit with her neuropsychologist, the doctor handed Christi a piece of paper and a pencil. He instructed her to take the pencil in her hand, and continue to make a circle pattern on the paper until he told her to stop. When the doctor said, "Start," she began scribbling on the paper as hard and fast as she could, but certainly not in the shape of a circle. After about 30 seconds, the doctor ordered her to stop, but she made even stronger marks on the paper. The neuropsychologist gently reached down and removed the pencil from her hand.

Glancing at me with a worried look, he said, "This, quite frankly, is what I feared the most. There is no way to know if her brain will recover to the point where her mental processes will function properly." He continued, "Given her current state, I am not so sure that I would have the same Pollyanna[9] attitude that you have." Driving home from the doctor's appointment that day I prayed, "God, You can't leave her like this! Please heal her brain and all of her mental processes."

In the weeks that followed, it was obvious that God had released more of His healing virtue. The next time the neuropsychologist asked Christi to perform the paper and pencil routine, she did it just perfectly! What a relief!

Mrs. Santa Claus arrived a bit ahead of schedule that year. Karen, who attended our weekly womens' Bible Study, visited me one day at the hospital. As she was preparing to leave, she requested that I give her my house keys. My rebuff was, "I don't want to give you my house keys, and you are not going to get my house keys." I had been home so infrequently that the inside of our house was in dire shape.

Quite uncharacteristic of Karen and her mild-mannered self, she gave me one of those firm motherly looks and said in a loud voice, "Give me the keys to your house!" Not wanting to make a scene in the hospital waiting room, I forked over my entire ensemble of keys in the little leather pouch that I carried inside my purse.

When I arrived home the following evening, my dear sweet Christian sisters had traveled to the desert and cleaned our two level home – all 2,400 square feet of it! They not only cleaned everything thoroughly but left little dishes of potpourri here and there, printed scriptures on cute-little hang up whitchits, deposited quarts of homemade soup in the refrigerator, and they even washed and folded ALL of the laundry. You name it. If it needed to be done, it was! I felt like the most professional cleaning service in all 50 states had just competed in a contest and I was the winner!

A couple of years later I had to call Karen one day and ask her how they got the surface area above the burners on my kitchen stove so clean as I just wasn't able to get rid of the gradew. Karen chuckled and said, "I don't know. I will have to ask my mother because she was in charge of cleaning that specific area of the kitchen for you."

On December 20th, as I was sitting by our daughter's bedside and listening to a popular worship song, I glanced over at her lying in the bed. She had her hands uplifted as she was attempting to praise the Lord. Suddenly, I noticed that she was no longer mouthing English words, but was praying in the Spirit. God had restored her prayer language! The Apostle Paul speaks of this in his letter to the church at Ephesus:

"And pray in the Spirit on all occasions with all kinds of prayers and requests. With this in mind, be alert and always keep on praying for all the saints." [Ephesians 6:18 NIV]

Jude, the brother of the Lord Jesus and of James, encourages us with these words,

"But you, dear friends, build yourselves up in your most holy faith and pray in the Holy Spirit." [Jude 1:20 NIV]

## Stirrings of The Spirit

Christmas Eve day, which was the 46th day of our battle, Christi was examined by her medical personnel, and it was determined that her vocal cords were no longer paralyzed as they were both now moving. Praise the Lord! That evening we held a little Christmas service in her room. Dan gave a little teaching from Isaiah 9:6-7 wherein it speaks of Jesus being called Wonderful Counselor, Mighty God, Everlasting Father and Prince of Peace. Our family communion time was celebrated with my husband's homemade matzo bread and grape juice. Prior to coming to the hospital, he had purchased some beautiful white candles to be placed in our silver candle holders so that we could have a candle light communion. We gave thanks unto God for our daughter's life and prayed for the family who had lost their daughter.

Our son made a little birthday cake for Jesus in the shape of a cross, decorated it with white icing, and sang "Happy Birthday" to Him. When Matty David was trying to get the candles in the correct placement that he desired on top of the cake, he pulled them out of one place in the frosting and then put them in another place which left holes in the top. When he saw this pattern he exclaimed, "These holes are just like the ones in Jesus' body when He was crucified!"

As Christi progressed with all of her various types of therapies, she also had to complete a basic life skills course in the hospital. In this area of the building, there was a little grocery store, restaurant, etc. so the patients could practice going to each one and ordering food or picking up supplies, making the correct change after paying for the items with pretend money and what have you. This was a most excellent exercise and test in basic math and social skills among others.

Now reentry into operating a motor vehicle was entirely a different story! I will never forget the day the instructor, Christi, and I merged onto the freeway after several successful completions of driving on short city streets. With our daughter behind the wheel and the ever so calm instructor in the front passenger seat, I was now the white-knuckled one sitting in the back seat holding on for dear life. Alas, we made it through this trial as well. Pills to raise low blood pressure were not required during that phase of recovery.

Christi's extensive therapy sessions continued, and she was finally discharged from the hospital on January 10th, 1992, after spending 63 days in the hospital. The rehabilitation staff gave her a little going away party complete with chocolate cake decorated with red roses and a message which read, "God Bless you Christi." Oh, and they also served vanilla ice cream along with the cake as they presented her with a loving greeting card with their personal messages. She had touched so many lives during her stay on both the sixth and second floors of the hospital.

As we were collecting all of her belongings to load onto the hospital elevator to take everything outside to put into the car for the drive back home, I noticed that Christi had something tucked under her arm. Upon closer examination, I discovered it to be a royal blue mat that she had used to prevent bed sores during her hospital stay. So in light of the prophetic word that I had received from God on November 11th, 1991 wherein He had said, "Take up your mat and walk," Christi literally walked out of the hospital with the blue mat rolled up under her arm. My only regret was that I did not have a camera handy to take her picture! I could not have orchestrated all of that if I had tried.

There may be those of you reading this book who may be thinking to yourself, "I cannot even relate to something like this and would not even know what to do." I would encourage you that when you encounter family or friends who are going through a similar situation, go before the Lord in prayer and ask Him to specifically show you what to do.

The Holy Spirit so beautifully engineered every detail of what needed to be done for our family. He may show some of you that you should go to the hospital and that others should stay home; that some should offer to clean the family's home or prepare meals, while others should care for the young children, or give money for gas and meals. The list just goes on at infinitum. By the grace and provision of our faithful God, everything that needed to be done and possibly could have been done for our family was done.

The high school from which our daughter graduated took up a collection of money and brought it to the hospital so that we could have gas money to drive back and forth as we lived one hour and 15 minutes one way from the trauma center. The day the school faculty members, students and their parents presented us with a large signed poster board containing their well wishes and the envelope of cash, I was so undone that I just turned my head to the wall and cried.

In all of the aforementioned, I have never felt so loved and blessed in my entire life.

Stirrings of The Spirit

Several years after Christi's accident, one of the nurses, who helped perform the MRI in the mobile unit in the hospital parking lot, served as a juror on one of my husband's court cases. At the conclusion of the trial, she waited inside the courtroom to speak with Dan. During their conversation, she told him that on the day of the MRI, Christi was so fragile that when they would change the IV bag of dopamine, Christi's blood pressure would drop to zero. The nurse also said that for years afterwards, when someone brought into the intensive care unit appeared to be in hopeless condition, those who had cared for Christi would say to each other, "Christi made it."

I would like to share with you a few things I learned through this time when our faith was tested to the maximum:

- There is a time to give to and a time to receive from the body of Christ. It is humbling to be on the receiving end; however, this was our time to receive. When we will not receive from others we short-change them and prevent them from being the blessing that God intended.

- God is not through using each one of us, and He is not through blessing each one of us.
- We are not to be afraid during the storms of our lives. In the gospel of Matthew 8:23-27, Jesus calmed the storm and admonished His disciples to not be fearful as He was with them. Likewise, Jesus will walk through every one of our storms with us.
- Do not doubt the prophetic words of the Lord. Every single thing the Holy Spirit spoke to my heart and said God would do was fulfilled in totality.
  - ❖ That the Lord of the Sabbath can heal on the Sabbath.
  - ❖ That God would heal Christi.
  - ❖ That she would take up her mat and walk.
  - ❖ That God would raise her up on the last day and He did indeed wait until the LAST day!
- Ruby's April 13th dream was fulfilled in that God had strengthened me, helped me and upheld me with His righteous right

hand during this ordeal. [Isaiah 41:10]
- John 14:8-15 speaks of believing on the evidence of the miracles performed by Jesus. I never thought that in my lifetime I would see a 20th century miracle equiva-lent to what Jesus performed when He walked the face of the earth.
- We are on God's timetable and not our own. In James 4:13-15 it reads, "Now listen, you who say, 'Today or tomorrow we will go to this or that city, spend a year there, carry on business and make money.' Why, you do not even know what will happen tomorrow. What is your life? You are a mist that appears for a little while and then vanishes. Instead, you ought to say, 'If it is the Lord's will, we will live and do this or that.' " [NIV]
  - ❖ The Old Testament prophet Jeremiah prayed in the 10th chapter and 23rd verse, "I know, O LORD that a man's life is not his own; it is not for man to direct his steps." [NIV]

- ❖ Shall we not also consult what the wisest king of all time had to say as well? In the book of Proverbs, King Solomon penned, "A man's heart plans his way, but the LORD directs his steps." [Proverbs 16:9] Or again in Proverbs 20:24, "A man's steps *are* of the LORD; how then can a man understand his own way?"
- We don't always get to choose what we are going to be able to do in our lives and/or what we can keep in our lives.
- The trials in our lives can be analogous to the emperor moth that has the flask shaped cocoon. While in the cocoon stage, the larvae would struggle **under pressure** to get through the bottle neck of the flask and emerge as a mature moth in order to be able to fly. One time, someone was observing the process of the moth trying to emerge through the bottle neck, and this person could not stand

to watch it suffer and struggle, so she clipped open the neck. The moth emerged all right, but it was never able to fly. It just kind of hopped along the ground. It was never able to attain full maturity because the natural process was interrupted. The same can be true of our lives – we will never emerge as pure gold if our tests and trials are helped along by some source other than what God has naturally intended.

- As the Apostle Paul so aptly reminded the church at Thessalonica, "So when we could stand it no longer, we thought it best to be left by ourselves in Athens. We sent Timothy, who is our brother and God's fellow worker in spreading the gospel of Christ, to strengthen and encourage you in your faith, so that no one would be unsettled by these trials. You know quite well that we were destined for them." [1 Thessalonians 3:1-3 NIV] It's quite a challenging thought to know that we are destined for our trials.

- The most important thing I learned pertains to God's sovereignty. One word: **sovereignty.** Respectfully, there may be some of you who have gone through something far worse than what I have shared or who have lost a loved one for which I want to say straight from my heart, "I am truly sorry for your loss."
  - ❖ Sovereignty means supreme power. A. W. Tozer writes, "God's sovereignty is the attribute by which He rules His entire creation, and to be sovereign God must be all knowing, all powerful, and absolutely free . . . Free to do whatever He wills to do anywhere at any time to carry out His eternal purpose in every single detail without inter-

ference.[10] The Sheila Fabulous (as I like to call myself at times) paraphrase of this is, "God does what He wants to do; how He wants to do it; when He wants to do it! It is His choice." Or another way of looking at it may be that "the defense team has rested its case in the matter." God does not have to defend Himself.

- ❖ As the Psalmist reminds us in Psalm 115:3, "But our God *is* in heaven; He does whatever He pleases." And again in Psalm 135:6 which reads, "Whatever the LORD pleases He does, in heaven and in earth, in the seas and in all deep places."
- ❖ King David reminds us in Psalm 139:16, "All the days ordained for me were written in your book before one of them came to be." [NIV]

- ❖ Three weeks before this accident, the mother of the driver, who is a Christian lady, was prompted by the Holy Spirit with these verses from Isaiah 57:1-2, "The righteous perish, and no one ponders it in his heart; devout men are taken away, and no one understands that the righteous are taken away to be spared from evil. Those who walk uprightly enter into peace; they find rest as they lie in death." [NIV]
- ❖ According to Daniel 5:23c, God *holds* our breath in His hand and owns all our ways.
- The emphasis is not on angels mentioned earlier in this chapter but upon God. It's not on how He did what He did but on what He did. Psalm 77:14 reinforces, "You are the God who performs miracles; you display your power among the peoples." [NIV]

## Stirrings of The Spirit

- When tragedy strikes, we need God, His son Jesus Christ and the Holy Spirit as well as our families and friends. We cannot carry the load alone. In our hour of need, Isaiah 61:1-3 is a powerful portion of scripture:

  "The Spirit of the Lord GOD *is* upon Me, because the LORD has anointed Me to preach good tidings to the poor;

  He has sent Me to heal the brokenhearted, to proclaim liberty to the captives, and the opening of the prison to *those who are* bound;

  To proclaim the acceptable year of the LORD, and the day of vengeance of our God;

  To comfort all who mourn, to console those who mourn in Zion,

  To give them beauty for ashes, the oil of joy for mourning, the garment of praise for the spirit of heaviness; that they may be called trees of righteousness, the planting of the LORD, that He may be glorified."

Jesus Christ had the Holy Spirit always resting upon Him without measure. He preached the gospel to the poor, the meek and the afflicted. He healed and bound up the spiritually and physically sick and brokenhearted.

Jesus broke the bonds of evil and proclaimed freedom from sin and satanic dominion. He declared the day of vengeance on sin and Satan, death and hell, and on all the powers of darkness, to be destroyed in order that we might be delivered.

To those who looked to Him for comfort, He freely gave and He turned their sorrow into joy.

Jesus is our comforter, preacher, healer and deliverer.

What do you or your loved ones have need of today? Do you have rivers that cannot be crossed? Any mountains you cannot tunnel through? **God specializes in things thought impossible.** I just shared with you an impossibility where God moved in a mighty way in our daughter's life.

Are you in any kind of storm today and brokenhearted, need freedom from captivity, long for comfort, desire to wear a garment of praise instead of despair? Jesus Christ can meet your every need. Call upon His name right now!

Sheila F. Eismann

## EPILOGUE – CHAPTER 1 – PART I

When Christi was moved out of ICU but was still on the sixth floor of the hospital, her neurosurgeon told me that she would never have the mental capacity to return to college. He said that he had never known of anyone who had intracranial pressure as high as hers who had the mental capacity to go to college.

Near the end of her hospital stay, a neuropsychologist tested Christi to determine the extent of her brain damage. After doing so, he told Dan and me: "This is really strange. I found evidence of damage to her lower frontal lobe that happened in the accident, but I did not find evidence of overall brain damage like you would expect from someone whose intracranial pressure was so high."

Interestingly enough, tomorrow, November 8, 2012, will be the 21st anniversary of Christi's accident. Many moons and many Junes ago I did not think that I would be working on this testimony to share with all of you as we approached this date. God always has a plan with a purpose.

As of the date of this writing, Christi is happily married with two beyond-adorable children. She completed her college degree, has a fantastic job, and is doing very well for which we are most thankful. In fact, she just completed four half-marathon races this fall.

I challenge each of you to be encouraged in the Lord and in the power of His might. He is the blessed controller of ALL things.

On December 16th, 2012, I drove to our daughter's house for a day of holiday baking with her and our granddaughter. Midway through the afternoon, I glanced down and saw Christi's white childhood Bible sitting on the kitchen counter. It was given to her on December 25th, 1983. I asked her if I could borrow it for a couple of weeks. When flipping through the pages, I found a handwritten message taped on page four. It was penned by the young daughter of the family who gifted this Word of God to Christi for Christmas that year. God was sending our second daughter a message seven years, ten months and eight days before her brush with death. No one knew it at the time except Him.

The taped insert reads:

"Mark 35-36 While he yet spake, there came from the ruler of the synagogue's house certain wich said, Thy dauter is dead: why troublest thou the master any further? As soon as Jesus heard the word that spoken, he saith unto the ruler of the synagogue Be not afraid, only belive Mark 5 35-36"

Only God, by and through the power of His Holy Spirit, could have moved upon the heart of a third- grader to write out these two verses by hand and tape them inside that little Bible all those years ago. Even though her spelling might not have been perfected at the ripe old age of eight, the word of God was alive and well within her spirit. This lovely young girl was moved by the Holy Spirit to put on paper what was residing deep within her without realizing the magnitude of her obedience.

I have included a copy of the young believer's admonition for your encouragement:

MARK 35-36

While he yet spake, there came from the ruler of synagogue's house certain wich said, Thy dauter is dead: why troublest thou the master any further? As soon as Jesus heard the word that spoken, he saith unto the ruler of the synagogue Be not Affraid, only belive

mark 5 35-36

Sheila F. Eismann

## EPILOGUE – CHAPTER 1 – PART II

When departing the local airport for her business trip in January of 2013, Christi purchased the January 14, 2013 edition of *Time* magazine which featured the concerns over Secretary of State Hillary Clinton's health. This related article highlighted Clinton's concussion and blot clot issues.

The opening paragraph of the above referenced article reads, "For most people, serious blows to the head don't occur often, but when they do, they can leave a legacy of damage. And despite sophisticated imaging techniques, brain-injury experts say such consequences, including sudden death, are difficult to predict."[11]

Stirrings of The Spirit

**2**

# YOU NEED TO SIT THIS ONE OUT

"If you make the Most High your dwelling—even the LORD, who is my refuge – then no harm will befall you, no disaster will come near your tent." [Psalm 91:9-10 NIV]

There may be times in our lives when we will be able to see the actual manifestation of Scripture come to pass, right before our lovely eyes. Such was the case on this warm early summer's eve of 1999.

A couple of months prior to this, I had gone through a major surgery, and my physical body seemed to be in no big hot hurry to heal completely. I had to just chill out and rest more frequently than I deemed necessary. For you see, this is quite a challenge for someone who is hardwired such as I am and whose personality would be described as more of a house framer as opposed to a finish carpenter. Not that one is any better or more efficient than the other as both are equally needed.

For thirteen consecutive years our family had attended a statewide conference connected with my husband's work. I looked forward to this annual event to see old friends, catch up on their familial news, meet new people, and on rolls the river.

In addition, our son was working on his Congressional Award, and one of the requirements was an expedition which was designed solely by the participant. Being the par excellent administrator that he was, our crown prince decided to maximize the upcoming trek and schedule a father-son backpacking trip into one of our state's gorgeous mountain ranges. Great idea!

During the formative stages of the newly planned trip, it was decided that since I was recovering from surgery, and my body was not 100% up to hiking and the likes, I would attend the three day conference and then catch a ride home with someone in attendance who lived in our valley.

Suddenly and without any forewarning,

## Stirrings of The Spirit

about ten days prior to departure, all of my desire to attend the gathering just disappeared. Initially, I attributed it to lingering fatigue.

About four days later the Holy Spirit impressed upon my spirit, *"You need to sit this one out . . . "*

My initial reaction was that of good ol' common sense and not trying to press the envelope by attempting to take in all of the activities that were normally a part of the conference. One of my father's favorite expressions flitted through my mind which was, "Now use your head for something besides a hat rack . . . Yes, Daddy, of course!"

The weekend of June 18th-19th was filled with the usual hustle-bustle of gathering up all of the backpacking gear, food, and so forth, in addition to the regular conference materials. With my ever lovin' and his hiking buddy leaving on Sunday afternoon, I settled in for a very relaxing week wherein I could just lounge in my pj's all day if I wanted to and Din-Din Morris would consist of tv dinners if I so chose. Wow, things were looking up already!

I spent a Magnificent Monday truly playing the part of a pampered queen, minus the soap-operas, but complete with good reading material, copious cups of tea, and the proverbial box of assorted chocolates. Not those gaggy ones with the cream filled centers because they are nowhere near as tasty as the ones with the nut centers. If what I needed was rest, then I had better get with the program. Alas, I convinced myself that I could play the part of a finish carpenter for a short while.

After relaxing for just a day and a half, I was beginning to notice that our little house was looking a bit too cluttered, to say the least. So about mid-morning Tuesday, June 22nd, I heard the Spirit say, "You need to get the house cleaned up as your men folk will be coming home early." In the natural state, I thought something would happen later in the week to cancel the backpacking trip.

The interesting thing is that for a period of about five hours following this, I had a sudden infilling of strength and energy that I had not experienced since March of 1999.

So, true to fashion, I donned my Hannah Housekeeper hat, gathered up my cleaning caddy, and strapped on the vacuum cleaner. Later that evening, a contented smile graced my face as I looked around at my domestic endeavors for the day. My attitude was, "Well, whenever my crew comes home, they can at least find their favorite chairs and a few clean dishes."

I read for a short while before retiring to

bed on the evening of June 22nd. At exactly 2:30 a.m., I was awakened from a deep sleep with an urgent command from the Holy Spirit to pray for safety on our cul-de-sac. Prior to moving to our house in 1995, I had never had such a compelling feeling, so I began to pray.

As I strained to hear something above my racing heart beat in the total darkness, the only thing that was audible was that of a slow moving vehicle as it made a full loop on our street. Total silence returned.

You can shake yourself if you think I could sleep a wink after all this. Forty-five minutes later, I heard what sounded like pots and pans being banged together. Getting out of my bed and looking out our master bedroom window, I observed our neighbor closing his side garage door and turning off the yard light. During this time, he worked from three o'clock in the afternoon until three o'clock in the morning, so it was not unusual for him to be performing his customary routine before sunrise.

Forty minutes later, I heard a sound similar to that of spray being released from an aerosol can. This went on for about ten minutes. When I could tolerate this no longer, I got out of bed and walked outside our front door.

Approaching the end of the sidewalk parallel to our house, I stopped dead in my tracks when I saw a black sports car parked perpendicular to our old brown hunting pickup, which we kept parked in our front driveway. The front bumper of the black car extended just past the pickup. All I could discern of the license plate number were the first two figures, so I knew that the car was from the same county as the one in which we presently lived.

The restraining power of the Holy Spirit and God's protective angels (Psalm 91:9-12) were obviously with me as I could not walk a step further and ran back into the house.

The second I frantically crossed the threshold, the driver of the sports car started the ignition and drove down to the end of the street. He then made a U-turn and drove back into the cul-de-sac again. During his second pass by our house he drove up onto our driveway, leaving black tread marks, and across our lawn before entering the north-south street once again.

Through all of this commotion, I was still unable to capture a complete license plate number. As a reed sways in the wind, I was imitating this motion inside our living room waiting to see if this unwanted visitor would make a third pass by our residence.

I phoned the local law enforcement

department who dispatched a very kind and compassionate officer to our home. He helped to allay my fears and develop a game plan until Dan could return from his conference.

It was only when I walked outside with the county mounty after the fact and before sunrise that I discovered my reflection could be seen in our neighbor's glass windows directly south of our house. So at approximately 4:00 a.m. when I ventured outside to see what was happening, the driver of the black auto could see my reflection in the window the entire time . . . Wow, angels watching over me!

So back to the original prophetic word that I received, ***"You need to sit this one out,"*** I am beyond confident to this day that it was the prudent choice to have made. Oh, and as for my mate and our son, yes, they did in fact come home early to a nice comfy and clean house. I felt badly that the adventure portion of the Congressional Award Program had to be shelved temporarily but am thankful for an understanding and compassionate family.

Suffice it to say, following this episode, we installed a security system in our house, and I obtained my concealed weapons permit along with a nice little black deterrent that measures about 4.5 inches high, 1.25 inches wide and 6 inches long. I think the brand name begins with an "R."

The thought did occur to me afterwards that most people who drive sleek black expensive cars, such as the one that left its calling card in our driveway and on our front lawn, have day jobs, unless of course they are enrolled in the five-finger discount program, own a midnite auto parts business, or are involved in the illegal use and/or delivery of various and sundry substances.

Sheila F. Eismann

# 3

# YOU'RE GOING DOWN!

"When you pass through the waters, I *will be* with you; and through the rivers, they shall not overflow you." [Isaiah 43:2]

As I turned my kitchen calendar from one month to the next in the spring of 2006, I felt a stirring from the Lord that I was to go back to all of the places that I had lived since being born, with the exception of my collegiate days, which were spent in another state. I continued to pray about this, and I knew that the Lord would show me when to go and what to do when I got to each of the respective locations.

On the 21st day of June, 2006, I sensed the Holy Spirit prodding me to go within the next two days which would have been on Friday, June 23rd. In preparation, I spent the day of the

21st fasting and seeking the Lord. I checked in my prophetic symbolism book titled *Biblical Mathematics, Keys to Scripture Numerics*, to see what the number 23 meant only to discover one word which was - - - **death**.[12]

Early the morning of the 23rd, en route to my birthplace, as I approached milepost 62, it was necessary for me to pull over to the side of the road and stop as there was a funeral procession in progress traveling toward me. The date was immediately quickened unto me again being that of June, the 6th month, and the 23rd day thereof. Six is the number representing man.[13] With respect to the number 62, I had been given Psalm 62 as my inheritance word while attending a Graham Cooke Conference in Albany, Oregon, during the summer of 2003. For those of you who are unfamiliar with Graham Cooke, he is a prophet from the United Kingdom.[14]

An eight-minute drive down Main Street showed no sign of the hospital in which I had been born. The building no longer functioned in that capacity. My parents and two older brothers had been living in another state when in December of 1948 their house burned to the ground. My mother was pregnant with me, and the following spring my father and mother ventured northwest and settled in a little place

## Stirrings of The Spirit

down by the river. I was the first of their children to be born in this state. Amazingly enough, the farmer from whom my parents rented ground that year and the doctor who delivered me both shared the same last name which was Smith.

As I neared that same body of water on this particular morning, I could sense in my spirit a churning or struggling in the river even though my physical location was still a mile or so away from the actual body of water.

Earlier in the week, I had felt a sensation of physically drowning. It seemed as though there was a lot of spiritual activity in this river as I continued on my journey. Before departing the official city limits, the Holy Spirit had me prophesy and declare to the town, river and the surrounding area "death has no control over me." In the Old Testament we see examples of God's appointed servants prophesying to the land in Ezekiel 21:2, the mountains in Ezekiel 36:1, the breath in Ezekiel 37:9, and the altar of the Lord in 1 Kings 13:2, just to name a few.

My spiritual journey continued another thirty miles or so into a little community where my dad farmed after leaving my birthplace. As I was driving down this road, a doe deer jumped right out in front of me and ran into a corn field to my right.

## Sheila F. Eismann

I learned later in life that some families in this geographic area suffered horrific tragedies, unfortunately. In the little barn where my mother used to milk our dairy cows by hand, our landlord's son took his own life. A few short miles from there, one of the families lost a twin son in a drowning accident. Within relative close proximity to all of this, a farmer lost his life during beet harvest when a harvest truck backed over him. All of these events occurred in the geographic shape of a triangle.

When I drove into this triangular area, in the Spirit I could see angels standing on the surrounding hillsides playing banjoes. Once again, the Lord had me state various prophetic proclamations with the continuing theme, *death has no control over me*.

I started the first grade in a little school house very similar to the type described in the Laura Ingalls Wilder *Little House* book series.[15] All eight grades were taught in three small classrooms. The teacher had one of those old fashioned bells with a long handle that she would ring when it was time to come in from recess. Just parallel to the school house was a dry creek bed with some old willow trees along the edges. We children loved playing outdoors, and for me it was a little bit of heaven on earth.

Regrettably, I could only attend school

there for a few months as in January of the next year my family moved to a small farm a few miles across the state line. My June 23rd spiritual mission included going to the family acreage, the site of the old church where I was baptized, and the schools I had attended. The Holy Spirit declarations continued.

    I felt led to go down by the Snake River that runs near the town in which I grew up. I drove my navy blue Durango® down close to the river bank and got out of the vehicle. As I looked to my left, I noticed a cross grave marker upon which rested a beautiful fresh red rose accompanied by a white rose. Our high school colors were red and white.

    As I gingerly stepped down closer to the water's edge, I stopped cold upon observing a large white she-monster looking object emerge from the river. It was wearing a long white flowing robe with fringed long sleeves. I could only see this demon from the waist up. Interestingly enough, this fallen angel knew my name, and I could hear it saying, "Come on into the river, Sheila." I could feel the hair on the back of my neck begin to stand straight up. I did not address this principality. I did, however, make the prophetic declarations concerning my family members as I was led by the Holy Spirit.

From there I continued on to a house in which my husband and I had lived when we were first married, which was in another county. Again, I made the statements that were imparted to me.

When I arrived home late that same afternoon, I really did not know what to think as I had just gone and done what I felt the Lord was directing me to do. In many ways, much of it did not seem to make sense in the natural realm. Perhaps some of you can relate to all of this based upon the spiritual experiences that you have had over the years or the directives and/or assignments that you have received from the Lord.

It was also during this time frame that my side of the family typically held a reunion each year. Different family members would take turns hosting, so it would be in a different geographic location, which added to the enjoyment. For the 2006 gathering, it was the families living in our region who were to serve as the hosts and hostesses.

The festivities started on Thursday, July 6th, and continued through Saturday night, July 8th. One of the highlights planned for Saturday morning and into early afternoon was a rafting trip down the calmer stretch of the same river alluded to earlier in this chapter.

## Stirrings of The Spirit

We had rented three rafts from the local university. Eighteen family members signed up for this jaunt which meant six people would be riding in each inflatable.

Upon awakening early Saturday morning, the Holy Spirit began to drop into my spirit words such as breath, breathe, air and desperate. At first blush, I considered these to be a very different sort of spiritual message. These words just kept coming to me in droves and it was as if I could not shut them off.

After arriving at the little wide spot in the road complete with a convenience store, donning life jackets and lugging the three rafts down to the shoreline, our son-in-law, Scott, spoke with us concerning the trip in general, the safety measures, which rapids to watch out for, etc. My husband and two sons-in-law were designated as captains of the respective rafts.

The raft I chose was originally going to be all women with the exception of my better half. Suddenly, at the very last minute, my nephew, Andrew Lee strode over and announced that we would have the pleasure of his company for our adventure.

We navigated the first two sets of rapids without incident.

Immediately before coming to the third set of rapids I heard, *"You're going down!"* Having no clue what this meant, but sensing it was from the enemy, I countered with, "Get out of here devil. I am NOT going down!"

I recalled that a few months prior hereto, the Lord had quickened unto me to watch for 3's.

Our son-in-law, Mike, took his raft through first and had no problems.

In our raft, in the very front was my sister-in-law, Sharon; behind her and to my left was my middle sister; behind her was another one of my sisters-in-law; my husband was in the captain's seat; I was sitting to his right and then in front of me was my nephew, Andy.

We started into the rapids and within a couple of seconds, slammed into a large rock. I can remember being hurled into the back of Andy and then found myself trapped underneath the raft under water. I could not get my head out from under the raft despite repeated attempts to do so.

I started to swallow a lot of water and literally felt that I was drowning. I was fighting to get my head unstuck and suddenly it popped up from under the raft, and I grabbed onto the thin but very strong white rope on the side of the raft, all the while it was rushing down a very fast set of white water rapids.

This thought crossed my mind, "Does

anyone realize that I am missing, that I am not safely back inside the raft as of yet?"

My nephew, Andy, and sister, who were able to remain inside the raft the entire time, pulled Sharon back into the raft first, and by this time my husband had found my second sister-in-law in the water and was helping her back into the raft along with Andy's assistance.

I was really beginning to weaken in my upper body from trying to hang onto the rope in the fast moving water and could barely hang on. At that very crucial moment I heard my husband's sweet voice saying, "I'm coming; I'm coming." It literally sounded like the voice of Jesus. Thankfully part of Scott's initial raft trip instruction was to show each of us how to pull someone back into the raft to safety if necessary, so Andy reached down and fulfilled the initial instruction to a "T."

What I did not realize at the time was that when our raft slammed violently into the large rock, Sharon had been thrown over, head first, and my other sister-in-law had been tossed out as well, along with my husband. Despite the presence of many large rocks where Dan had been thrown out, he did not hit his head on any of them which might have rendered him unconscious at the time and prevented his successful rescue attempts.

According to our son Matt, who was in the third group waiting to navigate that set of rapids, our raft was literally standing upright in the water after slamming head-on into the rock. Everyone else in the raft with Matt was powerless to help as they were too far back from us waiting their turn and the water was moving very fast. Mike and the members of his raft were too far ahead of us to render any assistance.

It was literally a miracle of God that none of us drowned or was seriously injured as it all happened in a split second. I am beyond confident that God was the air that I breathed while I was under water. And I truly was desperate for Him.

An interesting side note is that our nephew, Andy, had just completed two tours of duty during our ongoing wars, having served thirteen months in Iraq and seven in Afghanistan. During that time, he had some close calls, and God spared his life so he could return to the United States. My husband and I would pray for him on our early morning walks. Upon returning stateside and deciding to sign up for the family's rafting adventure, Andy, at the very last minute hopped into our raft on the river, and ended up helping save my life. God works in mysterious ways.

Stirrings of The Spirit

I am reminded of 2nd Thessalonians 3:3 which reads:

"But the Lord is faithful, who will establish you and guard *you* from the evil one."

Obviously all the days ordained for me had not yet expired according to Psalm 139:16, Job 14:5 and 23:14.

At the conclusion of our family reunion, I was reminded of a word that was released by Prophet Dennis Cramer on March 13, 2006 pertaining to the upcoming summer months. It was titled "The Perfect Storm is About to Hit – June, July, and August of 2006." The following is the word from Prophet Cramer:

"The Lord God will do nothing [worldwide] unless He first reveals His secrets to His servants the prophets. (Amos 3:7)

May I be perfectly frank with you? This well-known verse has always made me a little nervous as a prophet. In fact, as a prophet, it's made me a lot nervous! Because I'm prophetic, everybody thinks I should know everything God is doing on a worldwide scale. Boy, are they wrong! Don't forget, the world is a pretty big place.

I'm frequently asked, 'So Denny, what's

God doing?' To which I answer, 'I have absolutely no idea.' This is usually not the answer they're expecting, but it is truthful.

Let me assure you that I'm more frequently 'in the dark' prophetically than you might imagine. If God's not showing me, I'm not seeing. In this sense, I am far more dependent on revelation from the Holy Spirit than most believers. When the prophetic switch is off, brother, it is off. However, when He turns the switch back on, I will occasionally see some powerful prophetic things.

Prophetically, I've 'Seen' Something Powerful!

I would like to submit to you for judging something I've seen for this summer, the summer of 2006. Of course, God will be doing many other things worldwide during this same time period which He has not revealed to me. Again, this is just my 'glimpse', and I'm very excited to share it with you now. So again, please judge this.

Sizzle, Sizzle, Sizzle!

My 'word in season' this month is actually quite short — short but sweet. The Lord told me that the summer of 2006 is going to sizzle. I mean really sizzle! It's going to sizzle with the supernatural. I believe the Lord has told me that, 'In ninety days (June, July, August) there will be ninety days of unprecedented supernatural activity worldwide.'

Get Ready, Get Ready, Get Ready!

Approximately 90 days from now, (June, July, and August) there will be a supernatural release from Heaven. It will be a 90-day 'rush' of Holy Spirit power similar to the original Day of Pentecost. This 'mighty, RUSHING wind' will release upon the worldwide church a sizzling 90-day period of...

- Unprecedented Worldwide Healings!
- Unprecedented Worldwide Signs!
- Unprecedented Worldwide Wonders!
- Miracles, Miracles, and More Miracles!

But even greater than this outpouring of healings, signs, and wonders will be an unprecedented worldwide release of miracles — 90 days of genuine miracles of all kinds, miracles of all shapes, and miracles of all sizes. The summer of 2006 will be a season of sizzling worldwide miracles that are unprecedented, unparalleled, and unmatched:

- Unprecedented Worldwide Miracles Coming!
- Unparalleled Worldwide Miracles are Coming!

- Unmatched Worldwide Miracles are Coming!

The Lord would say, 'There will be an unprecedented worldwide release of miracles. All nations shall know that I am God!'

The Perfect Storm Is On Its Way!

So beloved, enjoy the next 90 days--there will be 90 days of 'calm' before this wonderful supernatural 90-day 'storm' of miracles strikes the earth. The perfect storm is on its way! People will be changed, cities will be changed, and nations will be changed! Get ready!"

Dennis Cramer, Dennis Cramer Ministries[16]

This prophecy was fulfilled in many ways which you can check out for yourself by accessing http://www.elijahlist.com/words/display_word.html?ID=4648. I submitted my fulfillment to the word on October 21, 2006. While the majority of the miracles listed at this site pertain to healings, I deem that my testimony would still fall into the "Sizzle, Sizzle, Sizzle" category. Granted, I could not hear or see anything that made a hissing sound when in contact with heat, such as a drop of water on hot metal, but then again, I was completely immersed under water for what seemed a **VERY** long period of time . . .

Sheila F. Eismann

# 4

# YA'LL GOT A MIC-RO-WAVE?

"But God has chosen the foolish things of the world to put to shame the wise, and God has chosen the weak things of the world to put to shame the things which are mighty; and the base things of the world and the things which are despised God has chosen, and the things which are not, to bring to nothing the things that are, that no flesh should glory in His presence." [1 Corinthians 1:27-29]

Besides opening this chapter with an extraordinarily long sentence, one could argue that a simple kitchen appliance, which is most likely used daily in American life, just might not have as much status in the kingdom of God as others. However, we know that God's ways are not necessarily our ways, much less His thoughts. [Isaiah 55:8-9]

After accepting Jesus Christ as our personal Lord and Savior in 1983, my husband and I began to pray for our unsaved family members that they would have their names written in the Lamb's Book of Life before it was too late. [Revelation 13:8]

As Jesus was instructing His disciples concerning the kingdom of heaven, he spoke the following in the first 16 verses of Matthew Chapter 20:

"For the kingdom of heaven is like a landowner who went out early in the morning to hire laborers for his vineyard. Now when he had agreed with the laborers for a denarius a day, he sent them into his vineyard. And he went out about the third hour and saw others standing idle in the marketplace, and said to them, 'You also go into the vineyard, and whatever is right I will give you.' So they went. Again he went out about the sixth and the ninth hour, and did likewise. And about the eleventh hour he went out and found others standing idle, and said to them, 'Why have you been standing here idle all day?' They said to him, 'Because no one hired us.' He said to them, 'You also go into the vineyard, and whatever is right you will receive.'

'So when evening had come, the owner of the vineyard said to his steward, 'Call the laborers and give them *their* wages, beginning with the last to the first.' And when those came who *were hired* about the eleventh hour, they each received a denarius. But when the first came, they supposed that they would receive more; and they likewise received each a denarius. And when they had received *it*, they complained against the landowner, saying, 'These last *men* have worked *only* one hour, and you made them equal to us who have borne the burden and the heat of the day.' But he answered one of them and said, 'Friend, I am doing you no wrong. Did you not agree with me for a denarius? Take *what is* yours and go your way. I wish to give to this last man *the same* as to you. Is it not lawful for me to do what I wish with my own things? Or is your eye evil because I am good?' So the last will be first, and the first last. For many are called, but few chosen."

Technically in this scriptural context in the gospel of Matthew, the workers with the agreement represent Israel who had the covenants and the promises of God. Obviously those without the agreement represent the

Gentiles, who would achieve equality with the Jewish people when salvation was made available to all through believing faith in Jesus Christ. {Ephesians 2:11-18; Romans 11:16]

My dad had not expressed much outward interest in spiritual matters during the majority of his life. In fact, there were times when he seemed to push back quite hard in this area. When I would try to share some of the exciting things that God was doing in my life, his spirit appeared quite closed.

Around the time Daddy entered the eighth decade of his life, I asked him if he would be opposed to receiving a Bible for Christmas. For anyone who knew him, he did not like surprises and would start floating out ideas for his prospective gifts in about October of each year. In fact, it was basically very unwise to show up on the doorstep of our old farmhouse commencing around December 1st with-out the requested holiday item(s) in hand.

I was beyond elated when Daddy finally consented to my gift suggestion but, not surprisingly, it came with his stipulations which were that he wanted a King James Version only of the Bible and that he would read just the Old Testament. He did not like the New Testament for some reason.

Since he was beyond his prime when gifted

## Stirrings of The Spirit

with the new Bible, Dad liked to sit in the cozy living room of his little farmhouse and read a few pages. I like to think that as his physical body was being warmed by the wood burning stove, his spirit was being heated by the word of God.

There would be times when Daddy would call me on the telephone exclaiming, "I can't believe what I just read in the Old Testament! There is so much bloodshed, war, and strife."

It would be a few more years before I finally got the revelation that the reason Daddy was so opposed to spiritual matters is because he deemed that he had killed too many enemy soldiers during his military service and that he was unworthy of being forgiven for having done this. One of his favorite quotes after having served in the Asian Theatre during World War II was, "War is hell."

Periodically when I would inquire of my father as to where he was reading in the Bible, he would cite chapter and verse to me, so I knew that he was not just giving me lip service in this regard.

In January of 2005 Daddy developed pneumonia which ultimately necessitated him being placed in the local nursing home since my mother was physically unable to care for him. Having moved to our little family farm in

January of 1956, it was obvious that after 39 years, a new abode was in order. In addition, at this juncture of his life, my father basically needed around-the-clock professional medical supervision.

My mother's health began to deteriorate in August of 2006, and after also developing pneumonia, she was placed in a local care center about fifteen miles from where my father was staying. For the next three months I would take my mother for frequent visits to see my father. On September 14th, 2006, they celebrated their 68th wedding anniversary.

As time progressed, I sensed that Daddy's life here on earth would end very soon. While I trusted the Lord with my dad's salvation, I desperately desired to have it firmly settled in my heart before he died to know that in fact he would be going to heaven.

In the middle of September 2006, the microwave that was installed in our home when it was built in 1994 decided to go on the fritz, and on the 26th day of the month, it quit completely. That's when I discovered that I used the bloomin' thing far more on a daily basis than I realized. It was another one of the maids on my non-existent, non-benefit payroll, such as my washing machine, clothes dryer and dishwasher, just to name a few.

In addition, the handy dandy finish carpenter who installed the original microwave had prepared a place for it above the kitchen stove, sandwiched in between the maple cabinets with very little wiggle room to spare.

After securing the model number off the unit that was a goner, I called one of the chain stores with an outlet in our area deeming that they could assist me with a replacement model. The clerk suggested that I have their repairman come out and take a look at the existing unit to see if it could be salvaged, because after all, you know, that would be much cheaper. Like maybe a whole $20, right?

A couple of days later, the technician arrived with repair kit in hand, and after testing this, that, and the other thing, determined that the older model could not, in fact, be salvaged so I would need to purchase a new one. Sure, no problem.

So I placed the second call to our local retail outlet store and was advised that while they did not have that older model in stock any longer, they had perused their various catalogs and found one that would surely work out just fine for us, and we would be very pleased with the same. Sounds like a plan, Stan. It was their only model that would fit in the same space as the old one.

The brand spankin' new white microwave arrived in the warehouse of the retail store on October 5th, and the clerk gave us the one ringy dingy to let us know it was now available for pick up.

So with my ever lovin' in tow, we descended upon the appliance floor of the store to pick up our new meal zapper. My spirit had just soared during the day as I thought, "Perfect! We can take this thing home, get it installed, and life will be waaanderful again."

Since we picked up the unit on a Thursday, my husband deemed that it would be best if we waited until the weekend to install it.

During this time, we had been attending a small fellowship in our town that scheduled a weekly gathering in the hosts' home on Sunday evenings at 6:00 p.m. The plan this particular weekend was to start the appliance installation process around 4:00 Sunday afternoon, or so, as it surely would not take long, and then we could relax and enjoy the company of our friends during the gathering later that evening.

Well, not so fast, sports fans. When Dan began to place the new unit in the existing space, he readily determined that it was going to be quite a challenge to get it to fit within the confines of the lovely maple cabinet work. As previously stated, there was not much extra room. Actually, there wasn't any.

Dan continued to work on the existing space to make it a little larger so the new microwave would fit but it was slow going. Not to mention the fact that the unit itself weighed a bit more than a sack of sugar and was a bit cumbersome on top of that! There was really only room for one person to work. I offered my able assistance, but actually my expertise lies elsewhere. There are days when I deem that I still have not found it, but I am looking for it . . . In addition, my husband had to fashion one-inch-thick blocks of wood to be used as spacers to attach the microwave to the bottom of the cabinet above it.

The eight-day fireplace mantle clock bonged six times reminding us that it was now 6:00 p.m. and time for the meeting to start, which was three-and-a-half miles down the road. I asked my husband whether he wanted to just abandon the project short- term so we could attend our regularly scheduled fellowship or just try to push through and finish it that night. He opted for the latter.

Around 6:45 p.m. the telephone rang, and it was one of the shift nurses at the care facility where my father was a permanent resident. As soon as I heard her voice, I knew that something was wrong. She indicated that my dad was going downhill fast and that we needed to get to the nursing home right away.

I immediately called our Sunday Night Fellowship group and asked them to start praying. My husband, teen-age son, and I grabbed our jackets, jumped into our car, and headed down the highway. The care facility was one hour traveling time from our house, and thankfully the road conditions were good.

En route to see my father, I prayed and asked God to keep him alive until we could get there to explain the gospel message to him one more time and that his heart soil would be tenderized to receive it.

When we arrived in Daddy's room, he was not there. Within a few minutes the nurse returned pushing the wheelchair with him sitting upright, but slumped over to one side. When he saw the three of us, he seemed to rally a bit.

We waited on the Lord for what we sensed was the right time to broach the subject of Dad's salvation with him and to make sure his mental faculties were still functioning properly.

Thankfully my dad and my husband had a very good relationship from the time Dan and I began our courtship. Daddy had been so good to Dan and taught him how to hunt big game and shared his love for the outdoors with him.

Daddy, who was famous for his nick names, affectionately called my husband, "Counselor."

It was Dan who began the conversation regarding what happened to someone once their life on this earth ended. Dan reminded my dad that we had spoken of these things with him before. Once again, Daddy tried his usual mantra of, "Well, an old sinner like me could never be forgiven because I shot too many people during World War II." Dan explained that he too had killed enemy soldiers during the Vietnam War, and that God had forgiven him, loved him, and accepted him.

Dan, the quintessential teacher, patiently explained to my dad that Jesus died once and for all for the sins of all mankind.

He quoted Romans 10:9-13:

" . . . that if you confess with your mouth the Lord Jesus and believe in your heart that God has raised Him from the dead, you will be saved. For with the heart one believes unto righteousness, and with the mouth confession is made unto salvation. For the Scripture says, *'Whoever believes on Him will not be put to shame.'* For there is no distinction between Jew and Greek, for the same Lord over all is rich to all who call upon Him. For *'whoever calls on the name of the LORD shall be saved.'* "

We waited quietly for the next couple of minutes, and it seemed as though a supernatural peace filled the nursing home room.

Daddy looked up at my husband and said, "Are you sure about this?"

Dan replied with a firm, "Yes;" looked down at my dad and said, "So, would you like to make a decision concerning what we just talked about?"

Without hesitation Daddy said, "Yes, I am ready. Can you tell me what to say, and I will just repeat the words after you?"

So, as his 13th grandchild held his right hand and his first born daughter held his left hand while standing next to the sides of his wheelchair, my father accepted Jesus Christ as his personal Lord and Savior on Sunday night, October 8, 2006. Forever it was settled, and there was not a dry eye in the place. I cannot begin to express the joy that filled my heart and the relief that flooded over me. Each of us hugged my dad and expressed to him once again how much we loved him and how much he meant to each one of us.

One of my father's lifelong habits was to have a stack of yellow legal pads within reach which enabled him to write out mathematical equations, draw maps, make lists, and so forth. This night was no exception. Daddy's last request before we departed that evening was for my husband to write out each and every word that he had my father repeat after him. When Dad asked me to tape the yellow sheet of paper from the legal pad onto his wall so that he could show it to everyone who came into his room, I simply could not refuse his request, nor would I want to do so. Before leaving the nursing home and telling Daddy good night, I could see where a peace had also settled over my earthly father for his remaining days.

It was around 9:00 p.m. when we started back home, and there was a sweet silence for about the first fifteen minutes of the drive. We decided to traverse the back country roads to our home as opposed to traveling on the freeway.

As the glorious golden harvest moon was making its ascent into the night-time sky, I was reminded of the verse,

"It [the Davidic throne] shall be established forever like the moon, even *like* the faithful witness in the sky." [Psalm 89:37]

So once again, the God of the universe had proved Himself faithful beyond the shadow of a doubt, as He had done so many times before this. He is truly a Keeper and we can always put our faith and trust in Him, His precious son Jesus Christ of Nazareth, and the Holy Spirit.

During the remainder of the drive back to our house, we talked about how the Lord works in the most astonishing ways. Had my husband not encountered the lash-up with the microwave, we most probably would not have been home to take the call from the nurse. Our son had planned to be gone that particular Sunday evening with some of his friends, so he would not have been home to take the call either.

In a special way, it only seemed befitting that my husband, my son, and I were there that night in my dad's room inside the nursing home when he accepted the Lord. The years of driving the limitless roads in the mountains on their hunting trips afforded Dan the opportunity to share the gospel with my dad. Even though he remained in refusal mode during these treks, when the crucial moment of decision was at hand, the gospel message was not totally foreign to Daddy.

Every three weeks for ten consecutive years, my parents made the 35-mile trip from their little farm house to my front driveway so that I could take them to their medical appointments, buy their groceries at the Grocery Outlet Bargain Market®, take them to lunch, and of course, it was Daddy who chose where we would eat on most every occasion, but every now and then he let Mama or Matty David choose, but not very often. Since I homeschooled our son for the majority of thirteen years, he was Grandma and Grandpa's helper loading and unloading the grocery carts, filling the food trays from the all-you-can-eat-buffets at the various restaurants, and so many other everyday tasks. We needed the bond that had been forged over so many years on this all-important night.

When we arrived home that evening, yes, there sat the microwave in the middle of the kitchen floor, not yet completely installed, but in the scope of things, it was beyond insignificant. It was one of our dearest family friends from the South who, when pronouncing the word "microwave," drug out each syllable of the word. Hence, this chapter is titled "Ya'all got a mic-ro-wave?" This is literally how this gentleman talks in real life.

Twenty-eight days later my daddy suffered a massive non-bleed stroke and never regained consciousness. He died at 9:00 o'clock in the morning on November 13, 2006, which was our 24th wedding anniversary.

A few years after accepting the Lord, I began to pay closer attention to numbers. God is always into the finest of details, or so it would seem. The number eight represents, "new birth, new creation, or new beginning."[17] With Daddy's salvation taking place on the eighth day of the month, he truly experienced his new birth.

Jesus spoke of this matter when the ruler of the Jews, Nicodemus, came to Him by night:

"Jesus answered and said to him [Nicodemus], 'Most assuredly, I say to you, unless one is born again, he cannot see the kingdom of God.'" [John 3:3]

The number twenty-eight is symbolic of "Eternal Life"[18] and twenty-four is "The Priesthood."[19]

The Apostle Peter provides a direct contrast between those who believe in Jesus Christ and those who do not in 1 Peter 2:4-10 which reads:

"Coming to Him [Jesus] *as to* a living stone, rejected indeed by men, but chosen by God *and* precious, you also, as living stones, are being built up a spiritual house, a holy priesthood, to offer up spiritual sacrifices acceptable to God through Jesus Christ.

Therefore it is also contained in the Scripture,

> 'Behold, I lay in Zion
> A chief cornerstone, elect, precious,
> And he who believes on Him will by no means be put to shame.'

Therefore, to you who believe, *He is* precious; but to those who are disobedient,

> 'The stone which the builders rejected
> Has become the chief cornerstone,'

and

> 'A stone of stumbling
>
> And a rock of offense.'

They stumble, being disobedient to the word, to which they also were appointed.

But you *are* a chosen generation, a royal priesthood, a holy nation, His own special people, that you may proclaim the praises of Him who called you out of darkness into His marvelous light; who once *were* not a people but *are* now the people of God, who had not obtained mercy but now have obtained mercy."

Oh, and concerning that Parable of the Workers in the Vineyard business that I mentioned earlier in this chapter (Matthew 20:1-16), yes, Daddy had indeed entered the vineyard, just in the nick of time!

On a final note, the nurse who phoned our home on the evening of October 8th, 2006, attended my father's services at the local funeral home. When thanking her for taking such good care of my daddy and paying her respects on this final day, she made the most interesting comment, which was, "It was sure a good thing that you happened to be home on that particular Sunday evening when your dad took a turn for the worse, because I could not seem to locate your cellular phone number anywhere, only your home phone number . . ."

# 5

# THE CHRISTMAS SURPRISE

"And my God shall supply all your need according to His riches in glory by Christ Jesus." [Philippians 4:19]

How many of you know that Christianity is a life-long process? Yes, after initially accepting Jesus Christ as our personal Lord and Savior and being baptized, we become new creations. [2 Corinthians 5:17] However, it does take constantly walking with God to learn how to hear His voice and discern what it is that He desires to accomplish through us by the power of the Holy Spirit.

A mere nine short months after getting married, my husband and I visited a non-denominational church located about fifteen miles from our home. We had gone at the invitation of my brother who was giving his testimony regarding his own salvation.

During the following week, neither Dan nor I discussed the church service the previous week, but decided we would give it a whirl on Sunday number two. I mean, after all, could there be any real harm in doing this sort of thing?

This fellowship was a group of dynamic believers who welcomed us with loving arms, and, since we were mid-lifers by this point in time, much grace was extended to us, thankfully.

One month later, we answered a Sunday morning altar call for our own salvation and ended up attending that church for the next four years.

Approximately four months later, in keeping with one of our annual Christmas traditions, I was in our kitchen placing the hand-crafted, flavored chocolates, fudge, holiday cookies, and wild game salami onto individual ornamental plates. These were intended to be surprise deliveries as we enjoyed playing the "Secret Santa" role.

Since it was already past 6:00 p.m. on Saturday evening, December 22nd, and with the temperature dropping rapidly, I did feel a bit rushed. Perhaps I had forgotten to take my chill pill, which my daughter, Christi, reminded me daily that I needed during that time. It was as if there were a set of arms and hands behind me helping to load the goodies onto the plate and to not be overly concerned about how fancy the spread looked.

As I handed the seventh and final plate to Dan, I sensed that I needed to make another plate. Not a big deal. You know, make it just like the other seven. But who was it for? I did not have a clue. And then another impression came to me, "Get a $20 bill from your wallet. Take a piece of tablet paper and write the following on the piece of paper, 'I don't know who this is for, but you do!' Place the money inside the paper and put the contents inside a small envelope." These instructions seemingly came out of nowhere.

With the eighth batch of goodies tucked under my arm, I stepped out the front door and met my husband, who had just driven our car around the circular driveway to pick me up.

Now I must take a moment to tell you about this delivery mobile. It was a two door, dark green, long, sleek, Oldsmobile 98® with a 455 cubic inch engine under the hood. This thing could flat move on the highway. A gutless wonder, it was not! One really did not have to worry about filling the trunk with sandbags during inclement weather as extra protection for driving on icy roads, as this thing weighed a whole bunch. Now parking was an entirely different issue, so one just learned to plan to take about three spaces in the South 40 of any given parking lot. The previous owner had kept it serviced religiously every 3,000 miles and delivered it with maintenance book in hand. The original purchase price was $750 cash on the barrel head, a real bargain even in those days.

The only issue was that the gas gauge did not work. The needle just registered permanently at the half-way mark in the little dashboard square space normally intended for such vital information. In other words, there were times when you did not really know if you were driving on the top half of the tank or the bottom half of the tank. After all, you can't expect everything to be in working order with a used car! We were never successful at locating the replacement parts for this gauge, despite our repeated attempts. Since I could not remember the last time we put some petro in the tank, I sincerely hoped we could get the job done and return home safely. Not knowing exactly how much gas was in the rig and donning my Anna the Administrator hat, I suggested the delivery

## Stirrings of The Spirit

route to my capable chauffeur, and the Olds just seemed to glide effortlessly all across the countryside.

As Dan got out of the car to take the plate to Recipient Number Seven, the name "Shielda" was dropped into my spirit. Well, I knew only one lady with that name, and she just happened to attend the same fellowship as the rest of the "Gracers."

Having attended our church for just a few short months, we had not yet learned the last names of some of the folks. And trust me, there were certainly some unique names, no disrespect intended. I had considered myself a fairly good speller up until this point in time, but I did learn some new pronunciations.

When my husband returned to the driver's seat, I asked him if he knew where Shielda and her family lived. As only God can do, Dan had overheard two gentlemen in the congregation talking the week before and remembered that the directions to this residence had been part of the conversation. There are times when having a memory like a hawk comes in handy. This was prior to cell phones and some families did not have their home phone numbers listed in the local directory. It had not yet occurred to me to obtain one of the church-member address books.

Since Shielda was not expecting me, I really hoped that she would, in fact, be home for our surprise visit. I had not yet learned that if God directs us to do something, He is not going to leave us in a lurch. Of course she would be home!

After Dan parked a few feet from the front door, I got out of the Olds with the plate of goodies and white envelope in hand, trudged up to the front door, and rang the ding-donger. Sure enough, Shielda answered with quite a surprised look on her face.

Since it was approaching 9:00 p.m. by this point in time, I apologized for calling on her so late at night and handed her the plate of goodies and the envelope. After saying goodbye, Dan and I shagged it for home in the Olds.

Two days later, Monday evening, was a candlelight Christmas Eve service at the church. Since these were normally well attended, including out of town family members, it did not afford much of an opportunity for people to visit afterwards. Prior to departing the church, Shielda handed me a small white envelope which contained a short letter.

Unbeknownst to me, during the Saturday afternoon while I had been playing Connie Chocolatier and fashioning all of the homemade candies in my kitchen, Shielda had been talking with one of her neighbors who lived close by. The lady explained that they had recently fallen upon hard times and so wished that she had the money to buy a nice Christmas tree for her children. These particular little ones seemed to be more enthralled with a tree than the actual gifts underneath.

Right before Dan and I made the special delivery on Saturday evening, Shielda had been sitting on her couch praying for her neighbor lady and the darlings. She specifically asked God to supply the money for a nice Christmas tree for this family.

Since the currency featuring Andrew Jackson's face had arrived after what would appear to be normal visiting hours, Shielda waited until after church the next morning for her special delivery.

Shortly after the folding money changed hands, Shielda's ever enterprising neighbor dashed out early Sunday afternoon, just after the local tree lot had posted the sign, "Christmas trees – 50% off." So the little children did get their wish ------ a great big tree which they could decorate with their homemade popcorn garland and whatever else their little hearts desired. God's timing is impeccable, even in the smallest details of life.

Shielda has since gone to be with the Lord,

but it was through this little Christmas experience that I began to learn my walk with God. Just as a young child learns how to walk by taking baby steps with his or her earthly father holding on, our Heavenly Father will do the same for us. We can always trust Him. There is no doubt about it!

# 6

# ON THAT DAY, THE CURTAIN WAS GRAY

"Bless the LORD, O my soul; and all that is within me, *bless* His holy name! Bless the LORD, O my soul, and forget not all His benefits; Who forgives all your iniquities, Who heals all your diseases, Who redeems your life from destruction, Who crowns you with lovingkindness and tender mercies, Who satisfies your mouth with good *things, so that* your youth is renewed like the eagle's." [Psalm 103:1-5]

One hot early morning in July of 2007, as I sat across the living room from my husband eating my breakfast cereal, suddenly I received a vision from God wherein a gray curtain appeared and obliterated my view of Dan sitting in his recliner. In the next scene of the vision, a large hand drew back the curtain slowly, and my husband's color turned ashen. Instinctively, I knew something was terribly wrong with him.

Gazing intently at Dan, I surmised, "Honey, you don't look so good. Are you feeling alright?"

Before I could say another word, the large hand appeared once again and closed the curtain. I waited for a few more minutes to see if anything else manifested from the Holy Spirit, but that was all I received that particular day. I told Dan I wanted him to get a physical exam.

The initial consultation and lab tests conducted by our general practitioner showed that everything was fine with the exception of Dan's red blood cell count being a little low. The doctor suggested that the tests be repeated after three months.

The second set of lab results performed after the prescribed period of time showed a significant drop in Dan's red blood cell count. Well, I astutely added another female to my non-existent, non-benefit payroll named "Nurse Nancy," who threw it into high gear and rounded up a hematologist. He conducted a series of tests, all of which were negative. Finally, he scheduled a bone marrow biopsy in February. On that day, Dan's red blood cell count was back up to just slightly below normal. Because Dan did not have any symptoms, some people naturally have a slightly low red blood cell count, and the hematologist did not want to put my husband through a bone marrow biopsy unless it was necessary, he just told Dan to come back in six months to have his red blood cell count checked. Total peace had not yet returned to my spirit however.

In March 2008, Dan and I visited some friends of ours who lived nearby. They were hosting Michael Danforth of Mountain Top International,[20] a prophet of God who we had met previously. Quite late in the evening as we were departing and just as I stepped across the threshold onto the sidewalk outside, the Holy Spirit came upon Michael and he prophesied to me, "You have a miracle daughter, a miracle granddaughter, and you will have another miracle before the end of the year."

We certainly had a miracle daughter as outlined in Chapter One of this book. Keep in mind, however, that this prophet knew nothing of Christi's previous brush with death or that she was pregnant with her first child who was due that same month. God had shown me in a vision shortly after Christi conceived that our grandchild would be a little girl. In this futuristic prophetic vision, I saw a beautiful little girl with long light brown hair, and I knew in my spirit that she was four years old. She was all dressed up in her fancy clothes and dancing through the building where Dan worked.

When I heard this prophetic word from God's servant, my spirit soared as in my flesh I deemed the words, "and you will have another miracle before the end of the year," pertained to the healing of my back and right leg. I had undergone a surgery in November of 2007 for this part of my body, but it brought no relief from the pain.

Sure enough, a few days after Michael delivered the word of the Lord, Christi gave birth to a beautiful baby girl. However, there was still this enigma of the third miracle before the end of the year.

Spring flew by as we celebrated the addition to our family, and almost a full year had gone by since the day the gray curtain appeared.

Commencing the 1st of July, I accompanied my husband on a Whistle Stop Tour of some of the counties within our state, which ended on

## Stirrings of The Spirit

Thursday, July 3rd. That evening we stayed in a local hotel located close to the large river that runs right through the town.

Since we had sat so much during the day on Thursday, including all of the driving, as soon as we checked into the hotel my husband and I went for an evening walk, which included walking down by the river. While on this walk, my spirit began to stir, but there was nothing noteworthy that came to mind. I just felt an overall uneasiness.

On Friday morning, July 4th, 2008, Dan and I got up early and went for another walk. As we returned to the hotel, I began to prophesy and prophetically release into the spiritual atmosphere salvation through Jesus Christ our Lord, healing, hope, deliverance, and truth. Again, I felt something strange in my spirit, but could not pinpoint just exactly what it was.

Later that evening, my husband and I attended the annual fireworks show, which was always a very festive event. We were seated at a table literally three feet away from the canal of water and fifteen feet from the actual river itself. Between the canal and the river, which ran parallel to each other, there was a portable stage upon which the members of the surrounding area were performing patriotic songs.

Following dinner, Dan and I turned our chairs facing east so that we could watch and listen to the orchestra, which began playing around 9:00 p.m. This part of the program continued for about an hour until dark when the fireworks would commence.

As I was watching the symphony perform and singing along to the patriotic songs, at exactly 10:00 p.m., I received a vision wherein I saw a huge boa constrictor suddenly appear about forty feet high in the air behind the symphony. It only manifested for about fifteen seconds, opened its mouth wide as if to say, "Ha, ha!" and then suddenly disappeared into the river.

This creature was so large in the spirit that there was still part of its body in the water even though it had risen that many feet in the air. It appeared right in front of my line of vision, so there was no way that I could miss seeing it. My husband did not see the vision, however, which is what happens sometimes. Please refer to Daniel 10:7-8.

A confirmation, of sorts, followed in the local newspaper the next day with the headline, "Coral snake may be loose . . ." The article continued, "A potential deadly snake that can paralyze human breathing muscles may be on the loose . . ."[21]

Stirrings of The Spirit

There is a Biblical account of a demon speaking in Luke 4:31-34 [NIV]:

"Then he [Jesus] went down to Capernaum, a town in Galilee, and on the Sabbath began to teach the people. They were amazed at his teaching, because his message had authority.

In the synagogue there was a man possessed by a demon, an evil spirit. He cried out at the top of his voice, '**Ha**! What do you want with us, Jesus of Nazareth? Have you come to destroy us? I know who you are—the Holy One of God!'

'Be quiet!' Jesus said sternly. 'Come out of him!' Then the demon threw the man down before them all and came out without injuring him." [Emphasis mine]

We returned to our hotel room around 10:30 p.m. Since my nighttime hygiene routine takes a bit longer than my husband's, Dan was already in bed when I decided to turn out the lights and call it a day. Suddenly, Dan experienced violent chills and the bed began to shake in the hotel room. This went on for about ten minutes, and just as I was ready to take him to the emergency room of the local hospital, his chills went away and the shaking of the bed stopped.

The next day, Dan had a pain in his side, and over the weekend it moved around to the front of his abdomen.

On Monday, he went to the doctor who diagnosed his pain as a kidney stone. She scheduled a CT scan later that day to see how many kidney stones there were and their location. After the CT scan, the technologist told him the radiologist wanted to do another one with contrast because there was something he wanted to see better. Dan agreed, and a second test was performed. At the time, he did not know the significance of the request for an additional test.

The following day, Dan received a telephone call from someone who informed him:

- that he had the radiologist's report;
- that the CT scan revealed masses consistent with lymphoma;
- that he knew this information was something Dan did not want to hear;
- and that he was sorry.
- He then said, "Goodbye" and hung up the telephone.

## Stirrings of The Spirit

At this point in time, Dan did not know what lymphoma was, except that it was something one did not want to have. He went online to learn about it, and one website said that up to half of those who have it survive five years, depending upon the stage of the disease, which range from I to IV, with IV being the worst.

The next week, Dan had a bone marrow biopsy, a PET scan, and a spinal MRI. On Thursday, we met with his oncologist. We learned he had stage IV lymphoma. It had spread from his lower abdomen all the way up his spinal column to the top vertebrae in his neck; through all of the bone marrow in his pelvis, vertebrae, ribs, and sternum; and into his spinal canal, where it was pressing on his spinal cord in two places, causing the severe back pain he had been experiencing. The lymphoma was also wrapped around Dan's aorta and around the S-1 nerve root on his left side. The doctor told us that as far as it had spread without causing any symptoms, it was probably small cell lymphoma, which is very slow growing. He was going to be leaving town on Friday and said that my husband would start chemotherapy in three weeks after the doctor returned from his trip.

On Friday, we received a telephone call from another oncologist's office asking us to come see her at noon. When we met with that oncologist, she told us they had received the pathologist's report and that Dan had aggressive, large-cell, non-Hodgkin's lymphoma. She said that he would be starting chemotherapy immediately, although because of another test they wanted to do, it would not start until Saturday. We later learned that it had begun as small-cell lymphoma and then, after spreading throughout his body, had transformed into large-cell lymphoma.

We drove home after the doctor's appointment and settled in our living room. This would have been almost exactly one year to the day after the gray curtain manifestation. As I sat across the living room from my wonderful husband and looked at him, I cried until I had no more tears left. I knew that God was with me through His omnipresence, but I did not feel as strong heading into this battle as I did with the one outlined in the first chapter of this book concerning our second daughter. During the life and death struggle for Christi, Dan was right beside me helping to wage the warfare, and rendering encouragement every step of the way.

Dan inquired of God, "Does this mean that all of the days ordained for me have come to an end?" He added, as if God did not know: "This would not be a good time for me to die. Sheila needs my support right now, this is a critical time in Matt's [our son's] life, and there is more I would like to do in Your kingdom."

It seemed as though God responded, "How was the lymphoma discovered?" My husband then remembered that it was simply by The Almighty's intervention that it had been revealed. After he had the CT scan, the kidney stone symptoms went away, and there was no kidney stone. If all his days had come to an end, there would have been no reason for the fake symptoms of a kidney stone to reveal the lymphoma because he would have been dead within less than six weeks. He then prayed. His prayer was not, "God, why did this happen to me?" It was not, "God, heal me!" It was simply, "God, may You be glorified through this."

After the diagnosis, I remembered a prophecy I had received about Dan some eight months earlier at a women's conference. The prophecy was that Dan would go through a very difficult time, but in the end he would be closer to God. This helped me to reconnoiter somewhat and it is a good thing as I had to hit the ground running. Since Dan was so gravely ill, time was of the essence. The medical personnel's schedules seemed to be maxed out even before my husband's appointments needed to be made. Thankfully, he was worked into the daily routines so that he could begin his treatments. These just happened to be very early in the mornings. This did not pose much of a problem in the fall of the year, but the winter months were a different story altogether.

The first course of treatment was intravenous infusions, two weeks apart, with a drug combination called R-CHOP. There were some good things about the chemotherapy. After Dan's hair fell out, he did not have to shave. To stave off weight loss, he ate five times a day, and, per doctor's orders, he consumed high-calorie foods he had not eaten for years, such as whole milk and croissants. He would lose eight pounds during the week following each treatment, and then gain it back the following week before the next treatment.

Dan had total peace about going through the chemotherapy. In fact, he did not even view himself as being sick. His attitude was, "Well, this is just something I have to go through. If God wants me to go through it, I will do so with a smile on my face." During his weekly visits to the clinic, there were several times when the nurses said, "You're sure smiling today" or "What are you so smiley about?"

## Stirrings of The Spirit

The first bone marrow biopsy revealed that the lymphoma had altered the DNA in Dan's bone marrow. After he had completed the six R-CHOP treatments, his oncologist did another bone marrow biopsy. Although there was barely enough bone marrow to obtain an appropriate sample, due to the damage done by the lymphoma and the chemotherapy, the biopsy revealed that the DNA in his bone marrow was back to normal. One of his oncologists said it was miraculous.

Dan apparently was not responding to the situation as was typical of most cancer patients. During one of his early visits to his oncologist, he chided, "Dan, you could die from this!"

My husband responded, "I could die while walking across the street." Not wanting the doctor to think he did not appreciate all he was doing, during our next appointment he told him, "I spent two years in Vietnam. Every day I flew I knew I could die, but every day I flew I believed I would live. By God's grace, I made it through relatively unscathed. I have the same attitude about this. I know I could die, but I believe I will live. I have no reason to be pessimistic. I am receiving excellent medical care."

Day seemed to run into night and night into day during this time. I would load my precious patient into our car and head for the cancer treatment center early in the morning. After returning home in the afternoon, I would insist that we lay down and rest for an hour or so. And then the daily routines of caring for my husband would continue. God also blessed me with what seemed to be supernatural strength during this entire ordeal. It was as if I looked at the calendar and it was July 17th, the day Dan was diagnosed, and when I looked at it again, it was the end of the year! We experienced the goodness of God as His army kept us supplied and encouraged with scrumptious nutritious meals, prayers, notes, cards, phone calls and e-mails. In addition, we received treasured communications from people all across our wonderful state which ministered to us mightily. There is really something powerful about the human connections when any one of us is going through a trial or tribulation of any sort. God works through people for which I will be eternally grateful.

One of the new practical regimens that I instituted into our daily lives during these first critical months was juicing vegetables and fruits. This routine was suggested by our dear Christian sister Terrie. Her recommendation was initially sent via e-mail with a brief explanation of the benefits of the process wherein she asked me to pray about introducing this into our lives. After I had prayed about this matter, I sensed a peace from the Lord so I asked Terrie to come over and give me the one easy lesson on juicing.

Terrie is one of those women who spread laughter and joy wherever she goes, and the day she arrived with a large cardboard box in her hands was no exception. It overflowed with organic fruits and veggies. Thankfully, Christi had spotted a juicer that just happened to be on sale the previous December and suggested that I purchase it. She commented, "I think it would be good for you to buy this [the juicer]. You never know when you will need one . . ."

Since Terrie had prepared the fruit and veggie mixture for quite some time for herself, she had formulated a recipe of sorts that tasted oh, so good! Another added benefit to this whole exercise is that Terrie had scoped out the landscape and knew where to obtain the best organic produce for the project. This fact alone saved me beaucoup valuable time.

Each batch that I made was just enough to be consumed by my husband and me before there was the risk of any type of harmful bacteria forming which can happen if it is allowed to sit for a lengthy period of time.

There seem to be strong proponents on

either side of the issue of whether or not juicing of fruits and vegetables is healthier than eating whole fruits or vegetables, but I must say that within a very short while after drinking my daily glass of the mixture, I had a lot more energy than normal. Perhaps the preparation time required for juicing may have served as a diversion of sorts as it gave me something to do and think about other than my husband's battle with lymphoma.

During my early morning prayer walks, I discovered a "healing loop" of sorts. As I traversed this one particular cul-de-sac, I received a vision wherein I saw angels lining both sides of the street. Each one had a golden censor in his hand, and when I would walk and pray, the angels would step from the sidewalks into the middle of the street and release a bright orange hot liquid from the middle of the censor. The first time I witnessed this, I pondered in my heart as to why the healing substance was such a bright orange color.

On the very few days that Dan felt up to walking a few yards on the healing loop, I placed my left arm inside his right arm and began to call on the name of the Lord. When I did, the angels manifested in the spirit, approached my husband and poured the healing substance of heaven from their censors

## Stirrings of The Spirit

onto his back.

As near as I could determine in the natural realm, the reason this healing substance was bright orange was to counter the effects of Agent Orange® that Dan had been subjected to while serving our country during his two tours of duty in Vietnam.

A short while after Dan was diagnosed with cancer, Prophet Michael Danforth and his wife Lori made the 704-mile trip by car to visit us and pray as they were led by the Holy Spirit. They arrived early in the afternoon and stayed several hours before departing for home. After they had been here for about three hours, and as Lori was sitting in front of our fireplace and looking at our front door, she received a vision from the throne room of heaven. She saw blood being applied to our front door and prophesied that the destroyer angel would not enter our house and take Dan's life. The basic premise of this comes from the 12th Chapter of Exodus:

"Now the LORD spoke to Moses and Aaron in the land of Egypt, saying, 'This month *shall be* your beginning of months; it *shall be* the first month of the year to you. Speak to all the congregation of Israel, saying: 'On the tenth of this month every man shall take for himself a lamb, according to the house of *his* father, a

163

lamb for a household. And if the household is too small for the lamb, let him and his neighbor next to his house take *it* according to the number of the persons; according to each man's need you shall make your count for the lamb. Your lamb shall be without blemish, a male of the first year. You may take *it* from the sheep or from the goats. Now you shall keep it until the fourteenth day of the same month. Then the whole assembly of the congregation of Israel shall kill it at twilight. And they shall take *some* of the blood and put *it* on the two doorposts and on the lintel of the houses where they eat it. Then they shall eat the flesh on that night; roasted in fire, with unleavened bread *and* with bitter *herbs* they shall eat it. Do not eat it raw, nor boiled at all with water, but roasted in fire—its head with its legs and its entrails. You shall let none of it remain until morning, and what remains of it until morning you shall burn with fire. And thus you shall eat it: *with* a belt on your waist, your sandals on your feet, and your staff in your hand. So you shall eat it in haste. It *is* the LORD's Passover.

'For I will pass through the land of Egypt on that night, and will strike all the firstborn in the land of Egypt, both man and beast; and against all the gods of Egypt I will execute judgment: I *am* the LORD.  Now the blood shall be a sign for you on the houses where you *are*. **And when I see the blood, I will pass over you; and the plague shall not be on you to destroy** *you* when I strike the land of Egypt.

'So this day shall be to you a memorial; and you shall keep it as a feast to the LORD throughout your generations. You shall keep it as a feast by an everlasting ordinance.  Seven days you shall eat unleavened bread.  On the first day you shall remove leaven from your houses.  For whoever eats leavened bread from the first day until the seventh day, that person shall be cut off from Israel.  On the first day *there shall be* a holy convocation, and on the seventh day there shall be a holy convocation for you.  No manner of work shall be done on them; but *that* which everyone must eat—that only may be prepared by you.  So you shall observe *the Feast of* Unleavened Bread, for on this same day I will have brought your armies out of the land of Egypt. Therefore you shall observe this day throughout your generations as an everlasting ordinance.  In the first *month*, on the fourteenth day of the month at evening, you shall eat unleavened bread, until the twenty-first day of the month at evening.  For seven days no leaven shall be found in your houses, since whoever eats what is leavened, that same person shall be cut off from the congregation of Israel, whether *he is* a stranger or a native of the land. You shall eat nothing leavened; in all your dwellings you shall eat unleavened bread.'

Then Moses called for all the elders of Israel and said to them, 'Pick out and take lambs for yourselves according to your families, and kill the Passover *lamb*. And you shall take a bunch of hyssop, dip *it* in the blood that *is* in the basin, and strike the lintel and the two doorposts with the blood that *is* in the basin. And none of you shall go out of the door of his house until morning. **For the Lord will pass through to strike the Egyptians; and when He sees the blood on the lintel and on the two doorposts, the Lord will pass over the door and not allow the destroyer to come into your houses to strike *you*.** And you shall observe this thing as an ordinance for you and your sons forever. It will come to pass when you come to the land which the Lord will give you, just as He promised, that you shall keep this service. And it shall be, when your children say to you, 'What do you mean by this service?' that you shall say, 'It *is* the Passover sacrifice of the Lord, who passed over the houses of the children of Israel in Egypt when He struck the Egyptians and delivered our households.' So the people bowed their heads and worshiped. Then the children of Israel went away and did *so*; just as the LORD had commanded Moses and Aaron, so they did.

And it came to pass at midnight that the LORD struck all the firstborn in the land of Egypt, from the firstborn of Pharaoh who sat on his throne to the firstborn of the captive who *was* in the dungeon, and all the firstborn of livestock. So Pharaoh rose in the night, he, all his servants, and all the Egyptians; and there was a great cry in Egypt, for *there was* not a house where *there was* not one dead." [Exodus 12:1-30] [Emphasis mine]

The vision Lori received and her prophetic proclamation concerning the destroyer angel helped to safeguard my spirit in the days that followed.

Dan's next course of treatment was four weekly injections of a drug called methotrexate into the spinal fluid of his lumbar spine. With each of those injections, it became harder to find a pocket of spinal fluid. During the fourth one, the doctor tried for about thirty minutes, moving the needle around in his lower back, repeatedly hitting the nerve going down his left leg, searching for a pocket of spinal fluid. It was fairly painful and excruciating to observe from a distance. The doctor decided to try another location, and during that short break the nurse came up to tell Dan she had to leave, but another nurse would take over. He was still lying on his stomach on the table, and she walked up, bent down, and said, "I have to go now. It's been nice meeting you. I hope to see you again sometime."

He smiled and responded, "It was nice meeting you too, but we can't keep meeting like this." His response took her aback, but then she smiled. It took another hour of trying in two different locations in his back, repeatedly hitting the nerve going down his left leg, before the doctor was able to complete the injection.

One side effect of the methotrexate was that the slightest cool draft on Dan's head would trigger a severe headache. When he was home working on his computer, he would wear a winter hat with ear flaps because even the slight draft of my passing by him would launch a headache. He purchased a black fleece beanie and wore it in the courtroom during oral arguments because his seat on the bench was below an air vent. The first time he wore it, there was a high school class in the courtroom. At the conclusion of the arguments, one of the justices went out to talk with the students. One of them asked, "Does he get to wear the hat because he's the Chief Justice?" The hat became known as the Chief Justice's Hat. When Chief Justice Roberts of the United States Supreme Court came to our state to speak at the law school, Dan presented him with a Chief Justice's Hat, but he said he would not wear it in court.

During his treatments, several of our Christian friends suggested that Dan fly to various places where there were healing revivals being conducted. However, the prophecy stated that he would **go through** a difficult time, not that he would be delivered out of a difficult time. When they made that suggestion, Dan would ask God if He had changed His mind. It never seemed that He had, so we did not travel to those revivals seeking a healing. Each and every prophetic word, irrespective of the number of letters contained therein, is vital when considering and fulfilling the same. Suffice it to say, the emphasis upon this particular oracle from God was on the preposition **through.** We were certainly not opposed to visiting a healing revival if that is what God directed us to do as there have been innumerable reports of people having been healed in these gatherings.

The next treatment was three days in the

hospital with an intravenous injection of a drug combination called R-ICE. It was uneventful, except for the hospital bed which was designed to prevent bed sores and had several air chambers that were continuously deflating and inflating by means of a loud air pump. At about ten o'clock the first night of his treatment, Dan asked the nurse if she could turn the pump off so he could get to sleep. She said there was no way to do it. He asked if he could unplug it, but she said he could not because it would also unplug the call button.

After trying in vain to get to sleep, my husband got out of the bed, fashioned a bed on the floor using several pillows, and went to sleep there. Fortunately, the IV tubing was long enough to reach that far. He awoke about an hour later with the nurse standing over him asking, "Sir, Sir, what are you doing?" He told her he could not sleep in that bed. She and her assistant immediately wheeled the bed out and wheeled in a normal hospital bed. Then he had a good night's sleep.

Following that treatment, they harvested stem cells from Dan's blood by inserting a catheter into his jugular vein and running his blood through a centrifuge (an apheresis machine). They wanted ten million stem cells, half to use and half to keep frozen in reserve.

Due to the risk of infection, the catheter could remain in him for only five days. Each day's harvest took about five hours while all of his blood circulated four times through the machine. Because of how badly damaged his bone marrow was, the medical personnel were concerned that they would not be able to obtain enough stem cells within the five days. By the end of the second day, they had collected eleven million. The woman operating the apheresis machine said it was a miracle.

Dan's last treatment before his stem cells were placed back into his body was six continuous days of intravenous infusions of high-dose chemotherapy with a drug combination called BEAM. It would attack all of the fast-growing cells in his body, including not only the cancer cells but the mucous membranes lining his mouth, throat, and entire digestive system. The side effects could include vomiting, diarrhea, and mouth sores and ulcers, along with hair loss and fatigue. He was told it would be seven days of getting really sick, seven days of being really sick, and seven days of getting better.

Another side effect would be the destruction of my husband's remaining bone marrow, so that his body would no longer be producing red blood cells (to carry oxygen), white blood cells (to provide an immune system), and platelets (to help blood clot).

The seventh day following the BEAM regimen, the medical staff would infuse back into Dan his previously collected stem cells in order to grow new bone marrow and a new immune system.

When Dan checked in at the nursing station to begin the treatment, the nurse asked, "Can I help you?"

He quipped, "I'm here for my three-week, all-expense-paid vacation."

She paused for a few seconds, then smiled and responded, "I'll take you to the Presidential Suite." She led him to his hospital room, but it seemed small for a prestigious suite.

Dan was connected to an IV the entire time. When he was receiving the high-dose BEAM chemotherapy, a semi-transparent brown plastic covered over the IV bag to warn others. The chemotherapy drugs were not only carcinogenic, but they were also toxic and would burn or damage flesh that they came in contact with. Dan thought the brown cover was appropriate when he would wheel the IV stand down to the first floor coffee shop for his morning latte. The first time, he told the barista that he needed a refill of his coffee IV.

Monday, December 15, 2008, was the date

scheduled for Dan's stem cells to be infused back into his body. I felt led by the Holy Spirit to take my camera to take pictures. A sweet young brunette registered nurse from a nearby town was on deck to administer the procedure.

Around 11:00 a.m. the remainder of the stem cell medical team entered my husband's hospital room to begin the stem cell reentry process. When one of the nurses removed the frozen plastic container from its container, I looked down, and lo and behold, the shape of the stem cells was that of a Christmas stocking. I just smiled and thought, "God, only You could do something like that!"

The fascinating part about a stem cell transplant using one's own stem cells is that the nanosecond the cells are reintroduced into the patient's bloodstream, each one instinctively knows where to go to begin growing new bone marrow. Please pull up a chair Darwinists as I will kindly debate any one of you on that issue . . .

God was very gracious during this treatment. Dan did not experience the severity of side effects that are common with this type of chemotherapy. Although his mouth became too sore for him to chew and swallow cottage cheese, he was able to find things on the menu that he could eat without having to resort to liquid or IV nutrition. After he had gotten through the worst of it, one of the nurses told Dan, "You're just sailing through this."

There was only one occurrence that caused the medical personnel concern. They tested my husband's blood daily to monitor his blood counts, one of which was his absolute neutrophil count (ANC). Neutrophils are the most common type of white blood cell and the body's first line of defense against infection. A normal ANC is above 1,500. When his dropped to 500, Dan was placed in isolation because at that point he had a severe risk of infection. When his ANC dropped to zero, he spiked a fever of 102°F. It broke during the night, but the next morning his oncologist said that Dan had kept him up that night.

The same Sunday evening that Dan was experiencing this high fever, I assumed that our son was packing his suitcase to fly home for the Christmas holidays since he was out of state attending college. The original plan was that I would pick him up at the airport Monday afternoon, December 22nd.

Late in the afternoon of December 21st, I received a call from Matt informing me that he had decided to drive home as opposed to flying. He reassured me with, "Don't worry Mom, I will be fine."

## Stirrings of The Spirit

As soon as I hung up the telephone I checked the road conditions from the Midwest to our home state and discovered they were challenging at best.

Around the dinner hour, one of the young women who attended our regular weekly church fellowship group just happened to drop by with a box chucker-block-full of all sorts of soup, bread, fruit, and snacks. Since I had just finished speaking with Matty David, I asked this young lady to agree with me in prayer that he would in fact make it home safely. As we held hands and prayed in our living room, I heard from the Holy Spirit, "I will arrest him in Montana." My co-prayer received a vision from God wherein she saw Matt wrapped in a protective bubble as he was traveling down the road. At the conclusion of our prayer time, I contemplated both of these revelatory downloads. It was not as if I did not already have enough with which to concern myself at this point in time . . .

I had tried to persuade Matt to stop overnight at a motel during his lengthy drive home, but he opted to press on through, despite the road conditions. Just as I crawled into my beddy-bye basket at 10:00 p.m. on that Sunday night, the telephone rang. Sure enough, it was Matty David on the other end of the line. He informed me that he had made a soft landing in a snow bank just outside of Monida, Montana. A truck was passing him during a heavy snowstorm, and when the driver saw an approaching curve, he just pulled into Matt's lane, forcing him off the road. According to our son, he had been traveling at a cautious rate of speed due to the road conditions, but the driver of the truck grew impatient after following him for a while and decided to pass Matt just before the curve in the road.

Alas, that was a pretty quick fulfillment of a prophetic word! Thank God that Matty David was not injured as his four-wheel drive vehicle just made a nice soft landing in the snow, and God's protective angels were truly traveling with him. By the time AAA fished him out of the snow bank, it was about 2:00 a.m. when he arrived at the closest motel to spend a few hours before continuing safely home.

Back to the prophetic word, "I will arrest him [Matty David] in Montana." When I initially heard it, the wording bothered my spirit. However, after consulting the dictionary, I felt a little better as one of the meanings of the word "arrest" is:

"to check the course of; stop; slow down: *to arrest progress.*"[22]

## Stirrings of The Spirit

While Dan was in isolation during his "three week vacation," he said he felt the way the Apostle Paul must have felt when he was in chains in Rome. He could not leave the room, but he was able to talk about spiritual things to some of the nurses who came in to attend to him.

For any of you who have had loved ones staying in the hospital during the Christmas holidays or been in there yourselves, you know that it can dampen one's spirit just a little bit. Armed with markers, poster board, scotch tape, stick pins, family photos and the like, I dialed up "Donna the Decorator" whose name is listed in my non-existent, non-benefit payroll. She met me in Dan's hospital room, and we had the most magnificent time transforming it into a Winter Wonderland, minus the snow, of course. I remembered some of the powerful Biblical scriptures that had ministered to me so mightily during Christi's hospital stay (please refer to Chapter One of this book) and affixed them to the walls. In addition, Matt had previously given his dad a set of IPod® speakers, which he had in his hospital room, so I cranked up his favorite praise and worship songs for all to hear, especially the angels in attendance. I don't think they are hard of hearing per se but may have been conversing in their own language concerning the peculiar wife of the bed patient ... (1 Corinthians 13:1).

Christi and Scott decided to pay Papa a little surprise visit two days before Christmas. When they arrived outside his Presidential Suite, Scott held nine- month-old Ali Faith outside the hospital room door window. When Dan saw her, his spirit soared, a big grin appeared on his face despite the severe mouth sores, and tears trickled down his pink cheeks.

My husband's oncologist just happened to be making his hospital rounds at the same time Ali Faith was peering into Papa's suite. He commented to Christi that "Dan was a man of steel," to which she replied, "The reason that he is a man of steel is because he has faith as steel."

During his rounds the following morning, the doctor commented to Dan that we sure had a beautiful daughter. This opened the door for him to tell his oncologist the miraculous story of Christi having been raised from the dead. At the conclusion, the doctor looked at Dan and said, "So what you are saying is that you prayed for her and she was healed?"

Dan, often a man of few words, replied, "Yes."

Opportunities such as the one I just mentioned are powerful fulfillments of

## Stirrings of The Spirit

Revelation 19:10d:
"... For the testimony of Jesus is the spirit of prophecy."

The testimony of Jesus refers to the witness about Jesus. Biblical prophecy looks to or is often dependent upon the work of Jesus Christ and/or its proclamation. [Luke 24:27; 1 John 5:10; Revelation 1:2, 9]

During those times when we need extra encouragement, it is most helpful to remember the prior works of God as outlined in His holy word.

At 10:30 on Saturday morning, December 27th, while eating cereal for breakfast, the brand made from oats and fashioned in little circles, I felt led to read from the Smith Wigglesworth devotional that my dear friend Jenny Lou had sent me earlier in the fall. The passage for that particular day encouraged readers to simply take God at His word. If we needed anything, we were to merely ask Him by faith, believing that what we asked for would be granted to us.

Well, fine and dandy there, Smith Wigglesworth!

At exactly 10:45 a.m., our telephone rang and the caller ID bar read, "Wigglesworth, MA," with the phone number being 208-642-4000. I didn't even know anybody in real life who dwelled in Wigglesworth, Massachusetts. This caller was number 27 in our "recent calls" list, which at the time only recorded 30 telephone calls in one block and then automatically deleted the previous calls and started all over again.

With this Wigglesworth call being numbered 27 on the morning of the 27th, I was beginning to get the big picture. Upon consulting my reliable Biblical symbolism book, I discovered that the number twenty-seven represents the preaching of the gospel of Jesus Christ.[23]

Before he started the six days of high-dose chemotherapy, Dan was told that it would be about four months before he recovered enough to return to work full-time. By God's grace, he was back to work full-time eight days after he was released from the hospital. In fact, because the hospital had Wi-Fi, he actually worked most of the days he was hospitalized, doing legal research and writing opinions. When a nurse told him that he had set a record for returning to work full-time after that type of chemotherapy, Dan told her, "I would have returned to work earlier if I had known there was a record to break."

Dan left the hospital on December 29th.

## Stirrings of The Spirit

Michael Danforth's prophecy of another miracle prior to the end of the year was fulfilled in totality with just two days to spare. We do not know why God had Dan go through this trial, but we know He had a reason. It may have simply been to be a witness to others.

James 1:2 says, "My brethren, count it all joy when you fall into various trials." One reason we can consider it "all joy" is because it gives us an opportunity to demonstrate our faith in God. To Dan, going through the chemotherapy without a smile on his face and a thankful heart would have been indicating a lack of trust in God. This did not take Him by surprise, and He could have ended it at any time. We knew He had a reason; therefore, we trusted in His love and goodness. Demonstrating our faith is often much more powerful than talking about it.

Even though we had never technically received a medical prognosis, God had been gracious to give us a spiritual prognosis before we realized that we needed it! We had the prophetic word from a pastor at the Women's Conference a few months prior to the diagnosis, the sure word of the Lord from Prophet Michael Danforth, and the accompanying vision received by his wife, Lori. In addition, during the times that I would find my faith wavering just a titch, the Holy Spirit would remind me of the vision of our four-year-old granddaughter dancing in the building where Dan worked. In order for him to still be alive when she turned four years old in March of 2012, my husband would indeed make it through this trial.

During the first month after he was out of the hospital, Dan had to wear a HEPA filter mask in public because of the risk of infection. I would like to share one of the incidents that Dan recalled with respect to the mask. "One day when I [Dan] was entering the employee entrance at the courthouse, I was wearing the mask and my Chief Justice's Hat. The security person monitoring the security cameras in the capitol area saw me and sent security personnel to the courthouse, thinking I was a terrorist, or maybe he just wanted to know, '"Who was that masked man?"'

A month after being released from the hospital, my husband had another PET scan to determine the effectiveness of the chemotherapy. It did not show any active lymphoma. After reading the report, Dan's oncologist became emotional and stated, "This is a far better outcome than I ever expected."

I posed the following question, "Would you say it's a miracle?"

After pausing briefly, the doctor answered,

## Stirrings of The Spirit

"It's a miracle." The oncologist then commended my husband for his equanimity (mental calmness and composure) throughout it all. He added, "It must have been because of your spirituality and life experiences."

I could not resist and replied, "No, it was because of his faith in God."

Dan added, "That's right."

Following Dan's discharge from the hospital and his return to work, I experienced yet another spiritual epiphany, if you will. For two years prior to my husband being diagnosed with Stage IV Lymphoma, when I would pray in the Spirit it sounded similar to a Chinese dialect. During the time-frame of diagnosing exactly what type of cancer had invaded Dan's body, his lab results were sent to a few different places throughout the country. Finally, a female Chinese pathologist was able to crack the code and determine the exact results. In my heart of hearts, I deemed that perhaps the two-year assignment of this particular prayer language may have yielded the above result. Who knows? Was this a mere coincidence? I rather think not because as soon as the diagnosis was made, that particular dialect disappeared and has not yet returned.

Sheila F. Eismann

# 7

# "HAIL, KING OF THE JEWS!"

"And they [the Roman soldiers] clothed Him with purple; and they twisted a crown of thorns, put it on His *head*, and began to salute Him, 'Hail, King of the Jews!' " [Mark 15:17-18]

Having been born third in the lineage of the Tribe of Wood, at the age of ten I became the oldest of us six children to live at home. My father had determined that my two older brothers would fare better if educated in a private military academy.

Daddy was an avid outdoorsman, and since I was his offspring closest to legal hunting age, I was drafted into his annual treks. One of Dad's favorite hunting buddies at the time was a fellow farmer named Hank who just happened to own a camper shell which was loaded onto his four-wheel drive pickup prior to opening day of antelope hunting season.

Daddy, having done his due diligence by insisting that I complete my .22 rifle instruction at the local National Guard armory, was far more excited about my initial hunting experience than I was.

The day before the season was due to officially open, Daddy and I collected our marginal gear and followed Hank and his wife Mildred to the wild blue yonder. Upon arriving at the perfect spot, the thought did occur to me, "Wow, there's a whole lot of nothing out here – except quite a bit of sagebrush and plenty of lava rocks." Oh, the joys of being a novice!

We arrived late afternoon, and the first instruction I received was to unload our sleeping gear from the back of our old pickup and make a bed on the ground. "Sure Dad, no problem." But not to worry, because with Dad's extensive military training during World War II, rest assured that he had learned to bark orders most efficiently. The second rapid succession command was to get some twigs and dried Juniper tree branches rounded up to build a campfire. The sun was rapidly disappearing on the western landscape.

After muckling onto the large dark brown

## Stirrings of The Spirit

tarp, which thankfully did not weigh as much as the hay bales that we bucked by hand during the summer months, I was to pitch it onto the ground and, "Eureka," it would magically land on exactly the right spot on nice soft ground. The basic idea was to make a "bedding sandwich," if you will. The upper portion of the tarp would be the equivalent of our ground pad, the marginal sleeping bags containing two blankets each were to be placed in the middle, and then the bottom half of the tarp was to be pulled on top of the sleeping bags. Oh, now this would surely suffice despite how low the temperature dropped during the night. However, one must remember that even in high desert regions, it can get rather chilly after the sun sets.

Of the two orders, I determined that collecting the necessary ingredients for the fire took priority, especially since there were not a whole lot of Juniper trees in sight. After all, we were making our camp down in Pronghorn country where this particular species of tree is not usually found in abundance. The Creator of the universe seemed to have designed it this way since the eyes of our intended trophies have a huge advantage compared to the human eye.

The first night's sleep was basically

miserable at best, for it would occur to me about 2:00 a.m. during the dark of the moon, that, "Sheesh! I really should have concentrated more on clearing the area of at least the large rocks before laying the tarp down and making our night-time sandwiches!"

Despite the unpleasant accommodations, I managed to drift off to sleep and was awakened around 5:30 a.m. upon hearing Hank open the camper shell door. I felt a sudden chill as I reached down to pull the sleeping bag closer to my chinny-chin-chin. Much to my surprise, I heard a crackling sort of sound. What was that? After reaching outside to touch the tarp, I discovered the blanket of white frost decorating the outer layer.

The call to breakfast did not have to be issued a second time. Hank had graciously prepared pancakes, bacon, and eggs for breakfast, realizing that all happy hunters need some hearty victuals for the task at hand.

I may be accused of being somewhat obtuse on occasion, and despite having been only the ripe old age of twelve at the time, it was not lost on me that dear, sweet Mildred was still resting comfortably in her toasty camper bed with the privacy shade closed, and that her dearly beloved is the one who had bailed out of bed early-thirty to welcome his guests. To her

## Stirrings of The Spirit

credit, however, Mildred had packed Henry's lunch the night before, which included six delicious pheasant-fat cookies complete with dried fruits and nuts, to be doled out the next day, three per hunter. I did not have the heart to inquire of Hank how many pheasants he had shot earlier that year to produce enough fat to enable Mildred to bless us with her culinary endeavors.

In addition, Mildred would have a nice warm supper for us each evening when we returned from thinning just a little bit more of the soles of our shoes on the lava outcroppings and packing our hunting rifles for umpteen miles. The only lash-ups that occurred during the Din-Din Morris evening drills would be if Mildred decided to be ultra-creative and mix three to four different varieties of canned soup together in one pot. For some unknown reason, Daddy did not cotton to this. I guess that he was not a lifetime member of the Hunger Makes a Good Cook organization.

But guess what? Before our second evening stay at the Splendiferous Sagebrush Motel, I was privileged to get a timely lesson on the proper way to make a level outdoor bed in the desert. Since both Daddy and Hank were successful at bagging their big game on the excursion, any unpleasant aspects were soon forgotten. Despite accompanying my father on several subsequent trips, the routine and equipment stayed pretty much the same.

With the aforementioned background, when my husband Dan and I married up, it was my desire to have a camper trailer complete with a Twilight Lounge so if I needed to get up in the middle of the night, I would not have to stumble around outside, with the aid of my flashlight, trying to drain the radiator.

Shortly before our tenth wedding anniversary, we were thrilled to be able to leave our old green tent at home when embarking upon our outdoor adventures. We purchased a used 13-foot camper trailer, but alas, it did not have a built in bathroom. But hey, things were looking up because we had now moved from the outside to inside accommodations! Gratitude is an attitude.

Prior to moving to the big city a few years later, we sold the little unit to another family so that we could finally purchase one with bathroom facilities. Never having owned a fifth-wheel, I expected that surely these could be no different than the bumper-pull type. The thing I had forgotten to take into account was the claustrophobia factor.

In those days and at that time, I was one-half inch taller than I am now    and the needle on the bathroom floor scale unit did not seem to register as far to the right as it presently does. It's all good, because I still weigh two pounds less than a piano . . .

Desiring to appear most appreciative of our new acquisition, I decided to not focus on the ceiling of the fifth-wheel when I would retire in the evenings during hunting season. I did request, however, to lay permanent claim to the outermost side of the mattress in the event I needed to bail out of bed anytime in the night season.

After owning this particular model for a few years, it was becoming increasingly more difficult for my six-feet-tall-plus husband to crawl up the two steps into the far side of the bed. Not to mention the fact that if he zoned out and lifted his noggin too high at any given time during the night, he might be sporting a knot on the top of his head the next morning.

With my patience growing a little thinner than normal, we made the prudent decision to sell the fifth-wheel and secure a bumper-pull as we deemed that everyone would be happier all the way around. This was still the era in which our son and his faithful companion, Molly Dog, were gallivanting around the countryside with us.

In order to placate our beloved hound, I

dreamed up a little ditty to sing to her when we would hit the road:

"Molly Dog, Molly Dog, you're so wonderful.
I love you.
Me and my Molly Dog too."

And then I would finish off the song with a couple of seal-barking sounds. You know, just for the special effects and all. Dogs enjoy these too.

It has often been said that animals understand far more than we can ever imagine. Such was the case, I would like to believe, with respect to Molly Dog.

No wonder Matty David sat in the back seat, arm draped around one of his best friends, wearing his head phones and listening to some other type of music as opposed to my Molly Dog Song.

The plan was to hopefully sell our existing fifth-wheel in the spring so that we could try out our new mobile unit before hunting season. Sagacious people are supposed to do these sorts of things.

Never at a loss for creative words, I formulated the ad for the local newspaper and knew in my spirit that God would have a buyer.

## Stirrings of The Spirit

Just because I was not partial to fifth-wheels did not mean that every outdoorsy type did not care for them.

After placing a call with our local newspaper and speaking with the advertising department clerk, I began to pray. Two days went by, and the potential buyer had not called the number listed in our ad.

Mid-morning of the third day, something along the lines of a victory chant of sorts was dropped into my spirit which played innumerable times in my head. The repetition included such words as fire, wind, Jesus, redeemed, king, hail, and Lord, just to name a few.

At 10:10 a.m. on the fourth day, the telephone rang, and it was a gentleman who was responding to our newspaper blurb. He wanted to see the unit first-hand, of course, and we made arrangements to meet him at the storage unit where the trailer was parked. When I asked for his name and phone number all I heard was the word, "Hail . . . The voice continued with, "and my phone number is . . . "

Caught completely off-guard by his name, I asked him to repeat it which he did. I queried, "Is Hail your first name or your last name?"

The slightly indignant voice on the other end of the line replied, "Hail is my first name."

I continued with, "How do you spell it? Just like 'hail' in a hail storm?"

The response came back, "Yes, 'hail' just like in a hail storm."

He told me his last name, but I was so startled that it flew completely out of my head.

True to form, the prospective buyer and his wife showed up at the precise moment of the agreed time to view the merchandise we had for sale. Based upon his actions, this was not the camper's first such unit he had owned as he crawled underneath and conducted a thorough examination. Hail and his wife took their time looking through the inside and asking pertinent questions. He indicated that they had just sold a larger trailer and were looking for something smaller. There was a small bit of dickering over the initial asking price, but believe me when I say we did not hesitate to agree to his final terms in short order.

For the next couple of years we took a break from our annual camping and hunting traditions, but found that we really missed our adventures so we beat feet down to one of the local RV dealerships in search of a replacement unit.

A salesman met us in the parking lot and asked us if there was a model or floor plan in particular that we were looking for, and I informed him that we had a general idea. I added that at least we knew what we didn't want this time around.

A veteran of thirteen years in the industry, the salesman asked us to follow him as he thought the company had something we might be interested in acquiring. Within less than 24 hours of our arrival at the parking lot, the dealership had taken delivery of a new unit that had only been used five times. The couple who purchased the unit had experienced an unforeseen event. Unfortunately, the wife had become gravely ill, so the couple called the dealership to see if arrangements could be worked out for them to return the trailer.

When we stepped inside the bumper-pull, my husband I and looked at each other and just grinned because it was exactly what we were looking for and knew in our hearts that only God could have worked out the timing of that out-of-town delivery.

Another fascinating part of this testimony is that years later when I was recounting the story to a dear friend of mine of how I had reccived the words included in the victory chant in my spirit right before the buyer called, she exclaimed, "You have got to be kidding me! Did you know that we bought Hail's bigger fifth-wheel from him right before he bought your smaller fifth-wheel?"

I continue to be amazed at God's intricate handiwork. Oh, and for the record, we are still enjoying our bumper-pull.  Happy trails everyone!

# 8

# THE BEATER WITH THE HEATER

"Now there was a certain disciple at Damascus named Ananias; and to him the Lord said in a vision, 'Ananias'.

And he said, 'Here I am, Lord.'

So the Lord *said* to him, 'Arise and go to the street called Straight, and inquire at the house of Judas for *one* called Saul of Tarsus, for behold, he is praying. And in a vision he has seen a man named Ananias coming in and putting *his* hand on him, so that he might receive his sight.' " [Acts 9:10-12]

In Chapter 5, I mentioned that we had at one point driven an Oldsmobile 98® which was the flagship model of the Oldsmobile division of General Motors.® The particular model that we owned was manufactured during what was known as the "eighth generation."[24]

Some years later, God decided to change the boundaries of our dwelling [Acts 17:26] to a much slower pace of life. The scenery was my all time favorite, complete with sagebrush, Indian Paint Brush, coyotes, and the picturesque War Eagle Mountain[25] which could be seen outside our living room window. The view was most glorious when the mountain modeled its winter snow cap.

The only unpleasant aspect of living down there were the scorpions, which would crawl inside our shoes and other dark places to hide, or the rattlesnakes which liked to stay as close to the house as possible. After praying and asking God to remove the diamondbacks from the close proximity of our solar envelope home, He was faithful to send a foul tempered old bull snake. There were times when I could watch it make continual circles around the perimeter of our home and front and back lawns, hissing all the while. For it was during this time I learned that with their nasty temperaments, even the rattlesnakes don't like to hang around bull snakes. Maybe that's where the term, "Meaner than a one-eyed snake" originated.

Just before moving even further south, we determined that we needed much more dependable transportation than our ol' Olds could provide, so we traded it in to a local dealership and purchased a 1986 gray Subaru Legacy®. A sense of relief flooded over me before my "Sheila Fabulous" was even dry on the contract considering there were no medical facilities where we were moving, and we still had young children at home. The occasion could arise wherein I would need the Subaru to double as my ambulance.

Our gray auto continued to be a most reliable vehicle, because there were times when even though the rest of the valley was covered with a blanket of snow, we still received enough way down yonder to make driving a challenge.

The closest town to where we lived did not have a grocery store, much less a gas station or car dealership that offered the lube, oil, and filter services. The nearest one was approximately 45 minutes from our house. We put some serious miles on that buggy, and one day, when driving to teach a weekly women's Bible study, I commented to Matty David that we were going to have to drive that car until the wheels fell off. Even though he was just a young lad at the time, he looked up at me with lecturing eyes as big as silver dollars and retorted, "If the car doesn't have any wheels, how can you drive it?" Yes, he did in fact inherit his father's logic.

For over seven years, straight-hand running, we took the car to the dealership for regular service and maintenance and had never had an ounce of problems. One day, as I was cruising down the highway, suddenly the orange low oil dashboard light began to flash. How could this be since I had just taken the car into the dealership a couple of weeks beforehand for its 100,000-mile standard service? I slowed down and pulled off to the side of the road, turned around, and headed back home. Within that short distance, a strange sound began to emit from under the hood.

The logical thing to do was to call the dealership and explain what the car was presently manifesting and to arrange to have it repaired. Upon speaking to the service manager, I received nothing short of a strong push back in terms of any liability on their part. I was informed that yes, we could take it back into the service department, but we had better have our thick wallet loaded with the floppy green stuff handy upon arrival. Leave the thin one at home. The meticulous service records would indicate that in our entire ownership of the vehicle, it had never been taken anywhere else except to the place from which it had originally been purchased for any type of work or service.

Instinctively, I knew that taking the Subaru back to this place was going to be an exercise in futility. Ya think? There was only one intelligent move to make at this point which was to call my long time good and trustworthy friend named Strong-Arm. Having been born and raised in the area, she would certainly know of a competent car mechanic that she could recommend. Why certainly! Not to mention the fact that she had the innate ability to stretch a dollar from here to Nebraska and back again and to make the buffalo bellow on a nickel before spending it.

As soon as Strong-Arm heard my dilemma, the answer rolled confidently off her tongue as her family had used this beyond proficient repairman for decades. And rest assured, this guy had received more authentic certificates for completing vocational and trade school courses in his field than the normal shade tree mechanic. No medals made of leather hung on the walls of his business.

In addition, Strong-Arm was not the type who would use just anybody to work on her vehicles. At one point during her first ten years of marriage to her valiant Vietnam Veteran husband, wherein no little ones had yet arrived, she had her eyes on a Pontiac Firebird® dubbed "The Blue Bird" which sold for a whopping five grand. Well, Strong-Arm did not get it. Upon seeing it year-after-year, she would continue to comment on this car.

Following nineteen years of wedded bliss, and the addition of a son and a daughter, the wife saw an ad in the paper for "Red Bird." She mentioned this in passing to her Prince Charming and suggested they go take a look-see which they did. With the passage of the years, Strong-Arm had no intention at this point of buying such a vehicle, but the family ended up driving over to where it was located. Upon arrival, they were most impressed with the car's condition and the fact that it was her Firebird, only in red in lieu of the blue model.

The seller was a young man bound for college who needed the cashola. Strong-Arm and her family chatted with him for a short while, thanked him, and departed. A few days later, while she was driving to where the desert meets the forest, her ever lovin' called the soon-to-be college student and offered him $2,500 for the car even though the asking price was $3,000. The owner of the car agreed to the terms, so Strong Arm's husband hustled over to the destination station to fork over $500 in greenbacks and the balance which was nineteen years of loose change carefully rolled up in paper coin holders and secured in two grocery sacks. The young man even offered to drive his newly sold auto to Strong-Arm's house where her honey hid it from her in the garage. When she returned from her short stay in the mountains and entered the garage, Strong Arm was speechless.

Thus began the era of Strong Arm's beloved "Ldynred." She was now the proud owner of a 1978 Red Pontiac Firebird!

Strong-Arm and her wonderful husband just celebrated their 41st wedding anniversary. It goes without saying that she married well. Now, back to the story at hand.

The long-standing repair shop referred to us was located by the railroad tracks under the city's underpass. When I entered the door, I was very impressed because it was more organized and cleaner than some American homes. One could literally eat off the floor, and to those of us who are neat nicks, there was a place for everything and everything was in its place.

The repairman discovered that whoever had completed the previous service on the Subaru had neglected to replace one of the bolts that attached the cylinder head to the motor block. He proceeded to try to fix it but cautioned that he thought some permanent damage might have already been done in that short of a period of time. It was my humble opinion that this gentleman definitely knew his trade and was not just fobbing me off or some such.

The work on the Subaru was completed to the extent possible with the caveat being that the mechanic had done the best he could under the circumstances, but was highly concerned about the future life of the Subaru. Well, this was not going to cut the mustard now was it?

Thankfully, at the same time that we had purchased the Subaru we had also acquired a most reliable Mazda 323®. The best part about this little puddle jumper was the 39-miles-per-gallon it achieved for regular highway travel. That aspect certainly helped with the family budget factor since my better half was a circuit court rider during that decade. At least we were not totally shanghaied and had some reliable transportation.

After driving the Subaru for another month or so, the original knocking sound in the engine became much louder. Strong-Arm's mechanic gave me a conservative quote as to how much it was going to cost to repair it, adding that, in his lifetime career, it was not unusual to see some

## Stirrings of The Spirit

Subaru engines purr like a kitten with no problems approaching at least the 180,000 – 200,000 odometer readings. Unfortunately, that probably was not going to be the case with our gray Legacy.

Simultaneously with all of this Subaru challenge, we had met a country western family with five little darlings who lived about four miles from us. They had started attending a church in the big city and invited us to visit the fellowship with them. We accepted their invitation and continued driving the extra distance each week for the next month.

One Sunday morning, during the praise and worship service inside the church sanctuary, I sensed the Lord directing me to sit down quietly for a few minutes. As soon as I did, I started hearing a very clear directive in the Spirit such as the one at the beginning of this chapter which was, "Wash your Subaru, vacuum it, locate the title, put it in the jockey box, list it in the upcoming yard sale, and drive it to your sister-in-law Diana's house next week. There will be a man who will walk into her yard at 9:30 a.m. next Saturday morning wearing a gray shirt, tattered jeans, tennis shoes and no hat. He will be carrying an envelope with twenty-one $100 bills in his right hand. Explain to him the problem with the car and that you have discounted it according to the repair estimate made by the mechanic. He will insist upon purchasing the car despite the knocking sound."

I could literally see this man in an open vision. I was able to hear and see all of this unfolding from the throne room of God despite the instruments playing and the parishioners worshipping all around me in the church building. Hope filled my mind, soul, body, and spirit and I felt as if I was soaring with the eagles.

Around the same time as all of this car business was transpiring, we had sensed that we needed to begin downsizing from where we lived in the desert. The horse trailer would have to go along with countless other items. Diana readily agreed to our selling some things in her upcoming early summer yard sale, including the car. For you see at this point, it was pretty much relegated to "A Beater with a Heater." The clatter from underneath the hood literally sounded like the beat of a drum.

Saturday morning dawned as beautiful as ever and we made the hour-and-a-half drive to where the yard sale was scheduled. Dan drove the pickup loaded to the gills with the soon to be treasures for someone else's household, and I followed behind in the Subaru, praying the whole way that I would arrive safely and on time to meet the mystery buyer.

When we drove into her cul-de-sac, and true to form, sweet petite "Di" had been up since about 4:30 a.m. flitting around in her cute little summer shoes affixing price tags to various and sundry items. Donned with her floppy summer hat, she greeted us in the driveway with her ever familiar, "Hi dear, how are things? Can I make you a cup of tea or get you a little snack?"

It felt as if a host of angels was helping us there that morning getting everything unloaded and priced in short order. We had shaved the time a little closer than we had originally planned. And for you ardent yard sale folks, it is not unusual for buyers to begin showing up as early as 7:00 a.m. for a sale advertised to commence at 8:00 in the morning with the request of "No early birds please."

There was brisk activity for the first hour or so with no time for tea, much less a snacky-wacky. Fortunately we had eaten a small breakfast sandwich earlier. Monitoring the upcoming anointed hour required a juggling act as things were selling like hot cakes. Di spent the first part of the morning inside her house as several women were interested in looking at her dishes and other kitchen items that had been advertised. Dan was out and about placing large "Yard Sale" signs on street corners, which left me with the Lone Ranger® act of meet and greet, final decisions on selling prices, making change, bagging up purchases, and whatever else is entailed in a robust yard sale.

A middle-aged couple had entered Di's yard and walked over to inspect a used double bed sized, cherry wood headboard that we were selling. The wife of the pair did not want to pay as much as we were asking for it. As I continued my negotiations, in my peripheral vision I noticed movement to my right side which flashed the color gray. I glanced down at my wrist watch and sure enough, it was 9:30 on the nose!

Since I could tell the couple was not really serious about agreeing to my bargain basement terms for the headboard, I excused myself and walked over to meet the man entering the yard wearing exactly the same clothes, minus a hat or baseball cap, that I had seen in the vision the previous Sunday morning. He was, in fact, carrying a small white envelope in his right hand.

Glancing up, I saw where Dan had just returned from distributing the yard sale signs, and since I had shared the word of the Lord with him, he joined me in the middle of the

## Stirrings of The Spirit

yard. The man, who I would guesstimate to be in his middle 30's, indicated that he wanted to look at the car that had been listed in the upcoming weekly yard sales. My blurb had been added at the last minute to the major things which Diana had listed for sale, and it read simply, "Used Subaru." No price had been listed.

Dan indicated that the car was parked parallel to the street and asked the prospective buyer to follow him. I tagged along as well. After unlocking the doors, Dan explained to the gentleman the short history of the debacle with the bolt having been omitted during the 100,000 mile service, the loud knocking noise and that we had set a price of $2,100 cash. The total asking price included a discount for what the guesstimated repair bill might be if one were to go that route. To our sheer astonishment the purchaser stated that he did not care one whit about the knocking noise underneath the hood. In fact, the more we tried to elaborate on it and apologize for the same, the more impatient he became. He looked up at me and said, "I don't care about the condition of the car. Here are twenty-one $100 bills in this envelope, and I want to buy it now. I walked all the way over here this morning and I intend to drive off in that Subaru." Ever the observant one, Dan reached inside the jockey box (glove compartment) and hauled out the title, signed on the line, and handed it to the buyer.

While walking away, I heard the Legacy's engine start up with the ever familiar knocking sound, and peace flooded my heart as once again, only God could have orchestrated all of this. We had made full disclosure of the vehicle's issues, and I rather suspect that somewhere down the road maybe this man was a mechanic or made arrangements for a new motor to be installed. Who knows?

Or perhaps we had just entertained an angel unwittingly. [Hebrews 13:2]

## 9

# FROM WHENCE IT CAME, IT SHALL RETURN

" . . . For your Father knows the things you have need of before you ask Him." [Matthew 6:8b]

Yes, as much as we love our little arrows, they eventually become full sized and must be released from the quiver. [Psalm 127:4] Since we did not live in a restricted area pertaining to the number of vehicles a family could own at any given time, some teenagers were willing to earn their own money in order to purchase one. The wild, wild West does have some inherent advantages in certain areas.

Such was the case when our son Matt was in his junior year of High School. He was gainfully employed at a local pizza joint, and, of course, his weekly gas bill was more than his net employment check, but at least he was enterprising and exhibited a work ethic.

After scouring any number of parking lots in the vicinity featuring just about anything one could imagine being passed off as "good used cars," we continued to strike out in terms of what Matt had been able to save up in order to buy his first automobile. The positive aspect to these daily exercises was that my naivety lessened considerably upon being introduced to such lingo as "tricked out cars", "clouded titles," and so forth.

Perusing the classified section of the local newspaper one afternoon, I spotted an ad for a 1999 Honda CRX®. No price was listed. I placed a call to the out-of-state number listed in the advertisement, and the male voice on the other end of the line explained to me that he had just moved into our area with his family. The sales pitch continued with the fact that the vehicle itself was owned by his son who would be sure to strike a great bargain with us as he was "Headin' outta Dodge" at his first opportunity.

The seller's father offered to drive the car to our home that very afternoon. Things were really looking up now as I began to mentally calculate how much time this was going to save me on a daily basis as my son's place of employment was 30 minutes one way from our house if virtually no traffic was cruising on that busy stretch of highway. This would surely allow for the distinct possibility of lowering my blood pressure by a whole bunch. Oh, yes! If it came to fruition, the newly acquired auto could definitely be placed in my asset column as opposed to my liability column.

The appointment was set for 4:00 p.m. which came and went. The thought did occur to me that since the man was unfamiliar with our area and might not own a GPS, he could experience some difficulty in locating our residence. About an hour later he drove up, jumped out of the car, and ran up to our front door. He apologized for being late and did offer the "I am new to the area" defense. I glanced down at the license plate for the first veracity check and sure enough, it had an out-of-state plate mounted on the front bumper.

Matt David and I walked outside to scope out the CRX and asked the pertinent questions, or at least as many as we could think of at the time, the most important being the asking price. Knowing how much money our son could pay for the car, there was still a gap that needed to be closed. I also sensed that the seller had given his father permission to just unload the car for whatever he could get for it.

Several minutes later, Matty David settled on the purchase price of $2,100, which was the exact amount of money he had on hand. There must be something about the figure of $2,100 and vehicles with respect to our family!

After the arrangements had been made to fork over the funds to the seller, Matt was now the proud owner of the little white car. And while I might have a little bit more free time on my hands every day, there was still the matter of vehicle insurance. Well, forget lowering of the blood pressure, to which I alluded to a few pages back. Since this was our one and only male teenage driver, had I ever set myself up for a shock! I had to ask the insurance agent to repeat the monthly premium three times before it finally sunk into my gray matter as to what the total figure would be. Yikes! Don't bother to schedule that Cancun vacation for at least the next ten years.

This little acquisition proved to be just the ticket for the next few months. It did lack one very important component, however, commensurate with Matt's preferred hobbies. The CRX was not a four-wheel drive rig that could ascend to the top of the local ski lodge when the roads were snow-or-ice covered.

## Stirrings of The Spirit

Does it really make any sense to live in a region where snowboarding is available on the Black Diamond Runs in the back country if you can't traverse the roads providing access to them? Surely not! One season of bumming rides from friends and riding the lodge's bus back and forth for his favorite outdoor sport was all it took for Matt to set his face as a flint. He purposed in his heart that before the next winter rolled around, he would be driving a four-wheel drive vehicle.

In the spring of the following year, our wonderful son asked me if I would once again implement my creativity and run an ad in the local newspaper to try to peddle his Honda CRX. I have never found advertising to be inexpensive, and this was no exception. It seems that no matter where or how we tried to sell this little car, it just was not coming together.

One warm spring afternoon, my dear sweet sister in the Lord, Beverly Joyce, paid me a long overdue visit. I had met Bev in 1983 in our local church, and, after volunteering our services, she and I had been placed on the same prayer chain. This was pre-cell phone and personal computer days.

The usual procedure was for the designated prayer chain person to take the calls of the

215

prayer requests and then call each prayer captain, who would in turn place a phone call to the next person on the line until it got to the very end. This method may sound archaic to some of you, but it was very effective, and God answered many of our prayers. The saints were very committed to petitioning the Lord on behalf of situations which were way beyond our control.

The prayer captain for our chain was a registered nurse named Lola. I was second on the list, and Bev was third. This practice continued for several years, and even though I did not see Beverly in person that often, I felt like I had known her my whole life since I spoke with her so often on the telephone. Bev had the distinct privilege of being born into a very strong Christian family, and I used to describe her as experiencing the Christian life while still in her mother's womb.

Beverly accepted my offer of making her a cup of tea, and we sat and visited on our living room couch for a couple of hours. It seemed like five minutes or less.

All of a sudden, the Spirit of the Lord came upon me, and I jumped up and shouted, "Bev, come out to the garage with me!" Those of you who know me personally can attest to the fact that there are times when I am not the calmest person on the planet.

Both of us hustled through the laundry room hallway and into the third bay of our garage where the CRX was parked. Bev shot me a quizzical look as if to say, "Where's the fire?"

I pressed the button to automatically open the garage door, all the while explaining that Matty David had been trying desperately to sell his little car, but not one person had expressed any interest in it. I asked her if she would help me by laying her right hand on the hood of the car, pray with me, and agree by faith in God that He would send a buyer.

Both of us prayed a short prayer initially, and then the Spirit of the Lord came upon me a second time and I turned 180 degrees, lifted my right arm in the air, and shouted (as if God is hard of hearing or something, which we know He is not): "I pro-phetically call forth the buyer for this car. And since the car was purchased from a man who lived in Utah, it will return to Utah from whence it came."

Bev, looking as shell-shocked as I felt, came back inside the house with me. Nothing further was mentioned with respect to the CRX. We visited for a while longer, and she headed home. I told her that I would call her and let her know who bought the car. She still had that dubious look upon her pretty face when she backed down our driveway.

Had I just put God to the test with this whole "Utah" business? There were two paid advertisement days left on our current running ad. I really sensed that we had activated something in the spiritual realm when we laid our hands on that Honda in our garage.

What I recalled afterwards was the account from the book of Numbers in the Old Testament wherein God miraculously provided plentiful meat for the Israelites in the wilderness.

> "And the LORD said to Moses, 'Has the LORD'S arm been shortened? Now you shall see whether what I say will happen to you or not.' " [Numbers 11:23]

Matty David had been finishing up his school work during the time of Beverly's visit. As he was leaving the house to put in his evening shift at the All-You-Can-Eat Pizza Parlor, I told him that Beverly Joyce and I had laid our hands on the CRX and called forth the buyer. I added one of those cocked-to-the-right-head-sternly looks that only a mother can give which sent the message, "Don't doubt me on this one."

Late in the afternoon on the last day of our

ad, which had been running in the newspaper, an elderly gentleman called and expressed an interest in buying the car. He stated that he was in his 70's and that he did not drive much except in his local neighborhood which was about 45 minutes from where we lived. We agreed to drive to where he was located so that he could take a look at the CRX and make his decision.

Both Matt and I had purposed that we were not driving that car back home again. I should have also known that he had already been driving around town scoping out the parking lots looking for his replacement vehicle. No grass had been growing under his two feet.

One of Matt's co-workers was gracious enough to swap work shifts with him so we could drive to our appointment the next afternoon. Matty David headed out in the CRX, and I followed him in our car. The directions led us to a large mobile home park which was like driving through a corn maze, but we eventually found the correct address. As we pulled closer to the mobile home number provided during our initial phone conversation, I noticed that there were three cars bearing similar license plates parked very close-by, and I wondered who owned these.

The elderly man answered our knock on

his front door and sauntered out to look at the car. He had quite the poker face and took his own sweet time inspecting the vehicle. He did not ask very many questions, so Matty David and I just stood there with our teeth in our mouths waiting for the gentleman's response. Fifteen minutes later we received our answer in the form of, "Well, I guess it'll do the trick. I only have $1,900 in my bank account right now, and I'm buying it for my grandson who is headed back. The only thing we've been waiting on is a set of wheels to get him down there and I guess this one will do the job. Can I write you a check?" To which Matt quipped, "Sure can!"

While the elderly grandpa went back into the house to fetch his worn leather checkbook, Matty David grabbed the title and signed it. As the final exchange was made with a check for a car title, I turned back around and said, "Sir, could I ask you something? Where is your grandson going to live?"

Flashing a big grin he replied, "Utah."

I could not wait to get back home and call Beverly Joyce to tell her the good news, and that the prayer we had prayed by faith the day she came over to have a cup of tea with me was answered.

And yes, God provided a nice red four-wheel drive vehicle in mint condition for Matt before the first snowflake fell from the sky that winter.

## 10

## "DEADLY TORNADO RIPS ACROSS OKLAHOMA"

" . . . and the Spirit lifted me [Ezekiel] up between earth and heaven, and brought me in visions of God to Jerusalem, to the door of the north gate of the inner *court,* . . ." [Ezekiel 8:3b]

Many moons and many Junes ago, well exactly 187 of them, I felt a leading from the Holy Spirit to go into our master bedroom and spend at least one hour in prayer. So on the 18th day of June, 1997, with my trusty clipboard, blank notebook paper, and blue pen in hand, I headed for the bed Fred at precisely 1:05 p.m.

I sensed that I was to spend this hour praying in the Spirit as opposed to the prayer model that I sometimes used bearing the acronym of A.C.T.S. which stands for "Acknowledging God; confession to God for sins of omission and commission; thanksgiving to the Creator of the universe and supplication for the things I deemed that we needed."[26] Not my greeds, just my needs.

Approximately forty-five minutes into my prayer time, suddenly the following vision manifested from the Holy Spirit:

I saw a large twister tornado moving across flat land. It was very high in the air. Then I saw newspaper headlines which read, "Deadly Tornado Rips Across Oklahoma."

The Spirit lifted me up in the air and I could see houses, animals and people whirling around inside the tornado. They looked like clothes spinning in a washing machine. [For similar accounts of someone being transported in the spirit, please refer to Ezekiel 3:14, 8:3 and 11:1.]

Everything visible to the human eye lay in shambles for miles around – houses, cars, personal belongings. I heard in the Spirit, "Even the souls of men." [Revelation 18:13]

In the wake of the tornado, I saw some of the charred wood from the houses where they had been burned and other smoldering fires. So

## Stirrings of The Spirit

in some of the affected areas fires must have been ignited when underground pipes broke. There were also explosions which could have been the result of natural gas lines erupting. [End of vision]

My spirit was troubled for many days following this revelatory download. I prayed and asked God who I should contact regarding this vision, if anyone. I remembered that Ruby's family lived in Oklahoma, so I penned a letter to her on June 19, 1997, in which I shared what I had seen in the Spirit. It went without saying that I would be on prayer assignment for the members of Ruby's family and others who would be in the path of this monster storm.

April 30th, 1999, 681 days later, as I was unloading the groceries from our car and walking through the laundry room into our kitchen, the empty washing machine basin registered in my spirit. Instantly I recalled the June 1997 vision of the tornado and the words "souls of men" flitted through my mind.

After the groceries were carried into our kitchen, I dug out my prophetic notebook from two years earlier and read the word from the Lord once again. My spirit remained on high alert as I could see those houses, animals, and personal belongings being carried in the air at a high rate of speed. My heart began to race. I sat down in my prayer chair and called upon the name of the Lord.

Exactly three days later during rush-hour traffic in downtown Oklahoma City, May 3rd, 1999, a deadly tornado ripped through the state of Oklahoma that witnesses said was at least half-a-mile wide and tore through the central part of the state wiping out neighborhoods, killing at least 24 people and injuring hundreds.[27]

The following related newspaper headlines covered the aforementioned tragedy:

- "Biggest twister tore mile-wide path through Oklahoma"[28]
- "Tornadoes kill 36 in Midwest"[29]
- "Tornadoes leave lives, homes in ruins"[30]
- "Tornadoes rip open Oklahoma City's wounds"[31]
- "Oklahomans begin to pick up the pieces of nature's wrath"[32]
- "Oklahomans will rebuild – Houses, businesses, towns in ruins"[33]

As I stand in my office preparing to finish this manuscript on a snowy Monday morning in January of 2013, I am looking through a pile of newspaper clippings sent from Ruby's family members in Sapulpa, Oklahoma, to her following the deadly tornado in May of 1999. Miraculously enough, none of her family members perished in this storm.

My heart is saddened for the losses suffered by many people when this tornado sat down all those years ago. There are times in our lives when it is better to trust God than to try to understand the "why" of things beyond our finite comprehension.

We take comfort from Psalm 139:16 which reads,

> "Your [God's] eyes saw my substance, being yet unformed.
> And in Your book they all were written,
> The days fashioned for me,
> When *as yet there were* none of them."

There are only so many days ordained for each one of us before God calls us home. He is large and in charge of all of those details. Our Creator *holds* each one of our breaths in His hand and owns all of our ways according to Daniel 5:23c. In light of this, it is incumbent upon us to live lives worthy of His calling and to make the most of every opportunity He provides in His kingdom.

## Sheila F. Eismann

When instructing the church at Corinth, the Apostle Paul admonished them with these sobering words,

"For we are God's fellow workers; you are God's field, *you are* God's building. According to the grace of God which was given to me, as a wise master builder I have laid the foundation, and another builds on it. But let each one take heed how he builds on it. For no other foundation can anyone lay than that which is laid, which is Jesus Christ. Now if anyone builds on this foundation *with* gold, silver, precious stones, wood, hay, straw, each one's work will become clear; for the Day will declare it, because it will be revealed by fire; and the fire will test each one's work, of what sort it is. If anyone's work which he has built on *it* endures, he will receive a reward. If anyone's work is burned, he will suffer loss; but he himself will be saved, yet so as through fire." [1 Corinthians 3:9-15]

# EPILOGUE

My prayer is that you have enjoyed reading these true-life testimonies. I would like to encourage you to start keeping spiritual diaries or journals if you have not already implemented that practice. Reflecting upon what God has done for each of us is so encouraging.

If you have never trusted Christ as your personal Lord and Savior, I sincerely hope that you would consider doing so this very moment. To bring Him into your life, you need to admit your sin and inability to save yourself and ask Jesus Christ to save you. Ephesians 2:8-9 tells us, "For it is by grace you have been saved, through faith — and this not from yourselves, it is the gift of God -- not by works, so that no one can boast." [NIV]

Jesus has promised to save all who desire to turn from their sins and call on Him in faith. The Bible also instructs us in John 1:12:

## Sheila F. Eismann

"But as many as received Him, to them He gave the right to become children of God, to those who believe in His name: . . ."

Sheila F. Eismann

# APPENDIX

To conclude this set of true testimonies, I deem it is important to go into greater detail concerning the three revelation gifts of the Holy Spirit listed in 1 Corinthians 12:4-11. These gifts are the word of wisdom, the word of knowledge and discerning of spirits.

"There are diversities of gifts, but the same Spirit. There are differences of ministries, but the same Lord. And there are diversities of activities, but it is the same God who works all in all. But the manifestation of the Spirit is given to each one for the profit *of all:* **for to one is given the word of wisdom through the Spirit, to another the word of knowledge through the same Spirit**, to another faith by the same Spirit, to another gifts of healings by the same Spirit, to another the working of miracles, to another prophecy, **to another discerning of spirits**, to another *different* kinds of tongues, to another the interpretation of tongues. But one and the same Spirit works all these things, distributing to each one individually as He wills." [Emphasis mine]

Writing to the church at Corinth, Paul said, "Now concerning spiritual *gifts*, brethren, I do not want you to be ignorant:" [1 Corinthians 12:1]

During its establishment phase, God did not want the church in Corinth to be ignorant concerning these matters, and His desire is no less for present day churches.

An important aspect to remember is the Holy Spirit distributes His gifts to each one individually as He wills. [1 Corinthians 12:11] Every single one of the spiritual gifts outlined in 1 Corinthians 12:4-10 is precisely just that, a gift which cannot be bought, traded, manufactured, contrived, manipulated, or you fill in the blank.

## The Holy Spirit gift of the word of wisdom and the gift of the word of knowledge:

"Before we begin our study of the gifts of the Holy Spirit, it is important for us to understand that in the scriptures there is a mingling of gifts, so much so that at times we may question just which gift (or gifts) is being manifested. This need cause us no real concern, for it must be remembered that all of the gifts flow from the same source, the Holy Spirit. If we are unable to identify exactly and classify perfectly, let us not be overly concerned. As humans it is our nature to draw neat lines of separation and classification, but when we seek to impose this practice upon God, we only frustrate ourselves and we may generate unnecessary confusion.

The word of wisdom and the word of knowledge are two gifts that often work together. Throughout the Old Testament when the prophets would prophesy, the word of wisdom and the word of knowledge would flow together (knowledge, and what to do about it.) In reading the prophetic books of the Old Testament, you will notice the phrase time and time again, "The WORD of the Lord came to _____ (name)." Examples of this can be found in 1 Kings 17:8; Jeremiah 1:4-8; Ezekiel 1:3; Joel 1:1 and Haggai 1:1.

In the New Testament, much of the writings of Paul, Peter, James and Jude are the word of wisdom and word of knowledge. Also, John's letters to the churches in Revelation chapters 2-3 are this mixture. The word of wisdom often comes with the word of knowledge so that believers in Christ will know how to apply that knowledge correctly. These gifts are two of the three gifts that 'reveal' something. We call these gifts revelation gifts because they consist of information supernaturally revealed from God. Each of these gifts is the God-given ability to receive from Him facts concerning something, anything, about which it is humanly impossible for us to know, revealed to the believer so that he or she may be protected, pray more effectively, or help someone in need.

The gift of the word of knowledge is supernatural in character. It is not obtained by logic, or deduction, reasoning, etc., or by natural senses, but by supernatural revelation through the Holy Spirit. It is the sheer gift of God. It is not essentially a vocal gift. It is received quietly and inaudibly within the person's spirit. It may become vocal when shared with others.

A basic definition of the word of knowledge: a fragment or small item of God's knowledge, supernaturally revealed to a person by the Holy Spirit.

An example of a spoken word of knowledge can be found in John 1:47-49:

'Jesus saw Nathanael coming toward Him, and said of him, 'Behold, an Israelite indeed, in whom is no deceit!'

## Stirrings of The Spirit

Nathanael said to Him, 'How do You know me?'

Jesus answered and said to him, 'Before Philip called you, when you were under the fig tree, I saw you.'

Nathanael answered and said to Him, 'Rabbi, You are the Son of God! You are the King of Israel!'

It is important to consider what the word of knowledge is not:

- It is not human knowledge gained by natural means.
- It is not human knowledge sanctified by God.
- It cannot be gained by intellectual learning, studying books or pursuing academics.
- It is not the ability to study, understand, or interpret the Bible.
- It is not a psychic phenomenon or extra-sensory perception such as telepathy (the supposed ability to be able to read minds), clairvoyance (the supposed ability to know things that are happening elsewhere), or

precognition (the supposed ability to know the future.)

The gifts of the Spirit defy human scientific explanation and are not acquired by ordinary educational processes. No amount of education or learning can produce them. They are not dependent upon innate human qualities. For example, the word of wisdom might be spoken by a person of even less than ordinary wisdom. They are not accentuated natural talents and abilities. The least talented or able may as likely be the agent through whom God works as the most intellectually endowed.

It is a subtle ploy of the great deceiver of our souls to attempt to humanize the supernatural and to reduce the spiritual gifts to the level of mere human endowments, talents, and learned or acquired abilities.

A word of knowledge may be revealed to a believer in any of the following ways:

- A sudden inspiration or a deep inner impression.
- A dream, vision, or picture seen through the eye of the spirit, with the interpretation of what is seen.

- Hearing the voice of God, or of angels, audibly or in the ear of the spirit.
- A living personal word from the Lord through scripture.
- The vocal gifts of the Holy Spirit such as tongues, interpretation of tongues or prophecy. [1 Corinthians 12:10]

Supernatural visions and dreams are usually the word of wisdom or word of knowledge in operation. Acts 2:17-18 reminds us of what was spoken by the prophet Joel,

> *'And it shall come to pass in the last days, says God,*
> *That I will pour out of My Spirit on all flesh;*
> *Your sons and your daughters shall prophesy,*
> *Your young men shall see visions,*
> *Your old men shall dream dreams.*
> *And on My menservants and on My maidservants*
> *I will pour out My Spirit in those days;*
> *And they shall prophesy.'*

The word of knowledge may not always be fully understood by the receiver or the hearers.

It can seem like it's a riddle or a mystery. In the seventh and eighth chapters of the book of Daniel, we read where the prophet was troubled in his spirit and the visions that were given to him disturbed him greatly. In Daniel 8:27b, God's servant was appalled by the vision and it was beyond his understanding.

Oftentimes God will use a word of knowledge to uncover sin, bring people to Him, give guidance and direction, minister encouragement or impart knowledge of future events. Some Bible scholars teach the revelation of future events to be the gift of the word of wisdom rather than the word of knowledge since wisdom usually pertains to what to do in the future.

If you would like to take the time to examine some examples of a word of knowledge in the Bible, I have listed a few from the Old Testament and the New Testament.

Old Testament:

- 1 Samuel 3:10-14
- 1 Samuel 10:17-23
- 1 Kings 19:11-18
- 2 Kings 5:20-27
- 2 Kings 6:8-23

## Stirrings of The Spirit

New Testament:

- Luke 2:25-26
- John 1:29-34
- John 6:60-61
- John 13:38
- Acts 5:1-11

Hosea 4:6a reminds us that God's people are destroyed for lack of knowledge. We definitely need the gift of the word of knowledge operating in our lives and churches today!

The word of wisdom is a flash of inspiration. It is a supernatural revelation sufficient for the occasion of the wisdom or purpose of God. It is the wisdom needed to meet a particular situation, or answer a particular question, or utilize a particular piece of information.

Once again, it is vital to consider what the word of wisdom is and is not:

- It is not natural wisdom.
- It is not the wisdom gained from academic achievement.
- It is not wisdom gained from experience.
- It is not even the wisdom to understand the Bible.

- It is given as the Holy Spirit wills (1 Corinthians 12:11).
- It is given for a specific need or situation.

A word of wisdom may be revealed to a believer in Christ the same way that I have listed previously for the word of knowledge.

It is helpful to know that we can pray for wisdom, understanding and knowledge. In Ephesians 1:17, Paul prayed for the spirit of wisdom and revelation. In Colossians 1:9, Paul asked God to fill the believers in the church in Colosse with the knowledge of His will in all wisdom and spiritual understanding.

The following are examples of a word of wisdom found in the Old Testament and the New Testament:

Old Testament:

- Genesis 6:13-21
- Genesis 41:33 with Acts 7:10
- Exodus 28:3; 31:6 and 35:26
- Judges 7:5
- 2 Samuel 5:17-25

New Testament:

- Matthew 2:12-15
- Matthew 21:23-27
- Luke 20:22-26
- John 8:3-7
- Acts 27:23-26"[34]

## **The Holy Spirit gift of discerning of spirits:**

"The third gift along with the word of wisdom and word of knowledge that reveals something is the gift of discerning of spirits. It has a more limited range than the other two because it is limited to the spirit world.

Sometimes this gift has been called the gift of discernment which is in error. It is the gift of discerning of spirits. It is not the gift of discerning people; it is the gift of discerning of spirits. There is a huge difference.

From our study of scripture, we learn that there are four basic categories of spirits in the spirit world which are as follows:

- God - John 4:24
- Angels – Hebrews 1:14

- Evil spirits, deceiving spirits and demons - Ephesians 6:12; 1 Timothy 4:1 and Revelation 16:14
- Man - Zechariah 12:1; 1 Corinthians 2:11a

A believer in Christ may be (1) operating under the inspiration of the Holy Spirit; or (2) expressing his or her own thoughts, feelings, and desires from his or her soul or spirit; or (3) allowing an alien spirit to oppress him or her and be bringing thoughts from that wrong spirit. An unbeliever in Christ may be completely possessed by an evil spirit. The gift of discerning of spirits immediately reveals what is taking place. This gift is given to know what is in a person and to know the spirit that motivates.

First, we need to define the word 'discern.' It is looking beyond the outward to the inward, literally, 'seeing right through', or 'insight.' In the gift of discerning of spirits it means to distinguish between good and evil spiritual influences.

The following three verses are a sample of how the word 'discern' is used in the Bible:

- 2 Samuel 14:17 – 'And now your servant [the woman from Tekoa] says, 'May the word of my lord the king bring me rest, for my lord the king is like an angel of God in discerning good and evil. May the LORD your God be with you.' [NIV]
- 2 Samuel 19:35a – 'I [Barzillai the Gileadite] *am* today eighty years old. Can I discern between the good and bad?'
- Ezekiel 44:23 – 'And they [the priests] shall teach My people *the difference* between the holy and the unholy, and cause them to discern between the unclean and the clean.'

Some Biblical scholars believe that if there are no visions, (actually **seeing** the spirit), it is not the gift of discerning of spirits, but rather the gift of the word of knowledge in operation. They reason that if one is informed about a spirit, but has no vision of the spirit, he or she would not **discern** it. In some cases a WORD comes first then a vision follows.

Through the gift of discerning of spirits, we can discern the origin of certain actions, teachings, and circumstances that have been inspired by spiritual beings. It is the ability given by God to know what spirit is motivating a person or situation. The gift allows a believer to detect and identify spirits and provides supernatural revelation of the unseen spirit world, both good and evil. The real nature of this gift is knowing and judging – never guessing.

The gift of discerning of spirits is not a natural critical spirit, insight into human nature, human shrewdness, character reading, fault-finding, psychological insight or even spiritual discernment. It is not a spiritual gift to uncover human failings. It is not the spirits of people who have died. It has nothing to do with spiritism or spiritualism. The spirits of departed human beings are not on this earth, and to attempt to contact them is forbidden. [Deuteronomy 18:9-12]

Discerning of spirits is needed primarily to reveal the source of spirits. The first and most obvious function of this gift is to reveal the presence of evil spirits in the lives of people or churches. However, it also functions to evaluate the source of a prophetic message, a particular teaching, or some supernatural manifestation. The person functioning with this gift will be able to tell whether the source of the message or act is demonic, divine, or merely human. The gift of discerning of spirits enables a Christian to pick out the source of gifts and messages that truly come from God. Humans cannot be in contact with or understand the spiritual realm except by the power of God or the power of Satan.

Although the gift has to do primarily with evil spirits, it also is the ability to detect the presence of the Holy Spirit. Visions, seeing Jesus or angels are also included in the discerning of spirits. If one only discerns evil spirits, then the Holy Spirit gift of discerning of spirits is not in operation.

Our natural discernment can be easily fooled. The gift of discerning of spirits is a means of protection from satanic deception. It is easy to confuse the words of the spirit of Satan with those of the Spirit of God. Satan counterfeits the beautiful works of God by creating an outward appearance which is similar to the real work of the Holy Spirit.

Satan is known as the deceiver [Revelation 12:9], the father of lies [John 8:44], and the serpent [Revelation 20:2]. All these titles signify the subtle, crafty deceptiveness which he uses to bring about evil whenever he can. Many times his counterfeit is so plausible that one will be entirely deceived unless someone is present who functions with the supernatural gift of discerning of spirits. If demon activity was always so obviously reeking with evil and wicked intent, as we tend to imagine, there would no use for this gift of the Holy Spirit."[35]

The following are examples of discerning of spirits found in the Old Testament and the New Testament:

Old Testament:

- Genesis 21:17-19
- Leviticus 19:31
- Deuteronomy 32:17
- Judges 13:3-7
- 1 Samuel 16:14-15, 23
- 1 Samuel 28:11-19
- 1 Kings 19:5-8
- 2 Kings 6:17
- 2 Chronicles 18:18-22
- Zechariah 3:1-2

New Testament:

- Matthew 1:20-21
- Matthew 16:23
- Luke 1:11-20; 26-38
- Luke 13:11, 16

## Stirrings of The Spirit

- Acts 12:7-10
- Acts 13:9-11
- Acts 27:23-24
- 1 John 4:1

Sheila F. Eismann

# OTHER RESOURCES AVAILABLE FROM AUTHOR SHEILA EISMANN @ www.sheilaeismann.com or Amazon.com

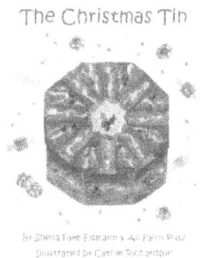

***The Christmas Tin*** is a most delightful read for the young at heart anytime during the year! This endearing book is based upon a true story featuring the older of the two authors when she was a young girl and conveys the timeless message that "love truly is the greatest gift of all." Children will especially enjoy all of the colorful illustrations contained within this treasure!

## Sheila F. Eismann

**RECOGNIZE YOUR CIRCLES**

A Humorous Look Into Life's Relationships

Have you ever wondered why you were the last one to hear of THE big social event of the year? Well, wonder no longer after reading this e-book titled **Recognize Your Circles**! When volunteering for an organization years ago, author Sheila F. Eismann was introduced to the concept of "the circles of your life." Since the idea was so beneficial to her, she decided to share it with all of you.

Straight From the Horse's Trough
Gardening Help for the Suburbanite and Urbanite

Sheila F. Eismann

**Straight from the Horse's Trough** is a humorous read to render assistance to the suburbanite or urbanite who desires to live a healthier lifestyle by growing his or her own food but is faced with the challenge of a small space in which to do so. This e-book is chock full of how-to steps and includes pictures to remove guesswork from the project.

Stirrings of The Spirit

***Freedom is Your Destiny!*** Vietnam Veteran Dan Eismann, using combat experiences to illustrate spiritual truths, invites you to take a journey with him as he presents a rock solid strategy for not only fighting your spiritual battles but winning the all important war. In the midst thereof, the most vital aspect is realizing you can experience freedom and become all that God has destined you to be!

Settle into your special reading spot, grab a cup of tea or your favorite meal, and plan to enjoy **Poetry Time** which is a wonderful collection of Acrostic and Traditional Poems.

Sheila F. Eismann

Everyone can use a little encouragement ~~ a dose of what is beneficial, ethical, and honorable. **Heart to Heart From God's Word** provides this for you. Penned with humor and wisdom, the daily tidbits are paired with Bible verses that convey life-changing principles which are designed for readers of all ages transcending cultures and continents. This devotional will challenge you to grow and fulfill your God given destiny. It doubles as a prayer journal also.

*A Woman of Substance* is a practical, interactive, and entertaining 12-week Bible study penned to help equip you fulfill your God-given destiny and impact the culture for Jesus Christ as the same time. It can be used as a stand alone study or devotional and works well in a group setting, too. It is designed for women ages Junior High through adult.

## Stirrings of The Spirit

  In Book One of The Sabblonti Series, **Jantzi's Jokers**, Jantzi Belle, matriarch of the Sabblonti family, has worked for decades to keep her cattle empire intact. Life takes a drastic turn when she receives a late night visitor. The brief disappearance of her Last Will and Testament could complicate matters between her daughters, Stormy and Sarita. Stormy and her husband, Chet Castins, are struggling to work through the loss of their three children. Against all odds, drifter Wyn Moreland makes a bold move when he decides that Sarita is his beauty to rescue. The county veterinarian, Dr. Ben Shaw, is also vying for her affections. Will Wyn emerge as the winner? Just prior to the dawn of the New Year, revelations come forth regarding forgery, cattle rustling, and land exploitation. Will the Sabblonti Empire survive, and more importantly, who will control its reins?

# Sheila F. Eismann

The Sabblonti Saga accelerates in Book Two of the Series, ***A Stormy Year***. Riding her high horse after inheriting the family fortune, Stormy Castins is determined to reinvent herself following her husband's accident. Blinded by jealousy, ambition, and naivety, she hires Less and Meg Alotto to oversee her vast high desert mountain domain. While Stormy is away, the cattle herd ends up in disarray.

Amidst the hot dry season, romance is blooming on several fronts despite a major showdown during a mid-summer celebration. The pesky Black Raven continues to wreak havoc at the most inopportune times.

Unable to overcome the vengeance which strikes by way of a mysterious range fire combined with the dire deeds of a cagey couple, the Sabblonti Ranch is in shambles just as Stormy starts to regain her senses. Humility is the prescription needed to open her eyes in order to realize what's really important in life. The sparks from a belated holiday rendevous set Chet and Stormy on their path to recovery.

# Stirrings of The Spirit

Desperation explodes when heiress Stormy Sabblonti Castins calculates her dwindling fortune in Book 3 of the Sabblonti Series, **Love the Tie that Binds.** Is she capable of learning the painful lessons of having to rely upon someone and something other than inherited wealth? As her husband, Chet, continues to heal from his near fatal accident, tormenting shadows of The Black Raven lurk in the background.

These high desert hills are alive with blessed babies, enchanting engagements, skillful scavengers, sophisticated scoundrels, rich revelations, timeless treasures, and western weddings.

The Main Sabblonti Ranch house abounds with an unexpected marriage, childrens' voices, and Sir Shelton sporting his silver bell.

In a captivating story of courage, trust, and faithfulness, will Stormy still be tied in knots or find lasting love by year's end?

Love, The Tie That Binds is the third book in The Sabblonti Series. Share the joys and sorrows of a mountain community in this swirling saga.

Sheila F. Eismann

Read and study with **Sheila Eismann,** Prophetic Author, Blogger, Speaker, and Teacher, in Volume 1 of her latest series titled ***Prophetic Insights for Daily Living.*** This **231-page** workbook can be used as a stand-alone devotional, individual Bible Study or in a group study. Sheila describes various dreams, visions, prophetic words, and teachings she's been given by The Holy Spirit from August 2020 through December 2020 which are designed to help you grow in spiritual knowledge and the operation of The Holy Spirit gifts. Each entry includes questions, contemplation, reflection, or a call to action.

Read and study with **Sheila Eismann,** Prophetic Author, Blogger, Speaker, and Teacher, in Volume 2 of her latest series titled ***Prophetic Insights for Daily Living.*** This **234-page** workbook can be used as a stand-alone devotional, individual Bible Study or in a group study.  Sheila describes various dreams, visions, prophetic words, and teachings she's been given by The Holy Spirit from January 2021 through May 2021 which are designed to help you grow in spiritual knowledge and the operation of The Holy Spirit gifts. Each entry includes questions, contemplation, reflection, or a call to action.

Sheila F. Eismann

Read and study with **Sheila Eismann,** Prophetic Author, Blogger, Speaker, and Teacher, in Volume 3 of her latest series titled ***Prophetic Insights for Daily Living.*** This **234-page** workbook can be used as a stand-alone devotional, individual Bible Study or in a group study. Sheila describes various dreams, visions, prophetic words, and teachings she's been given by The Holy Spirit from May 2021 through August 2021 which are designed to help you grow in spiritual knowledge and the operation of The Holy Spirit gifts. Each entry includes questions, contemplation, reflection, or a call to action.

## ABOUT THE AUTHOR

Sheila Eismann, author and publisher of fifteen books, is third in her lineage of five female published writers and poets. She endeavors to enhance the lives of others through education and encouragement via penning her inspirational and fictional books. Eismann, co-founder of Idaho Creative Authors' Network (ICAN), speaks at Womens' and Writers' Conferences.

Sheila invites you to check out her new website www.sheilaeismann.com and sign up to receive her blog posts and newsletters. Please send her an email at sheila@sheilaeismann.com to say hello and to let her know what ministered to you the most in this book or your favorite chapter. God bless, and Happy Reading!

Sheila F. Eismann

## *Where to find Sheila Eismann online and purchase her books:*

Email: sheila@sheilaeismann.com

Website: www.sheilaeismann.com

Facebook: www.facebook.com/sheila.eismann

Blog: "Prophetic Insights For Daily Living" www.sheilaeismann.com

LinkedIn: Sheila Eismann

Etsy:www.etsy.com/shop/BooksbySheila Eismann

# BOOKS BY SHEILA EISMANN

A STORMY YEAR

A WOMAN OF SUBSTANCE

HEART TO HEART FROM GOD'S WORD

LOVE, THE TIE THAT BINDS

JANTZI'S JOKERS

POETRY TIME – VOLUME ONE

PROPHETIC INSIGHTS FOR DAILY LIVING –
INSPIRED MESSAGES FROM THE HOLY SPIRIT
– VOLUME 1

PROPHETIC INSIGHTS FOR DAILY LIVING –
INSPIRED MESSAGES FROM THE HOLY SPIRIT
– VOLUME 2

PROPHETIC INSIGHTS FOR DAILY LIVING –
INSPIRED MESSAGES FROM THE HOLY SPIRIT
– VOLUME 3

RECOGNIZE YOUR CIRCLES

STIRRINGS OF THE SPIRIT

STRAIGHT FROM THE HORSE'S TROUGH

THE CHRISTMAS TIN

# Sheila F. Eismann

[1] "Paraclete." *Wikipedia*. Wikimedia Foundation, 27 Jan. 2013. Web. 06 Feb. 2013.

[2] Sper, David, RBC Ministries Discovery Series, (Grand Rapids, Michigan, Thomas Nelson, Inc. Publishers, 2002), PP. 4-5.

[3] http://www.youtube.com/watch?v=6BICo2eC8gI. N.p., n.d. Web. 06 Feb. 2013.

[4] "Golden Hour." *Merriam-Webster*. Merriam-Webster, n.d. Web. 06 Feb. 2013.

[5] http://www.eliyah.com/The Hebrew meaning for the word "vision" is the same one as used in Ezekiel 1:1 which is: **4759** mar'ah mar-aw' feminine of 4758; a vision; also (causatively) a mirror:--looking glass, vision. Web. 06 Feb. 2013.

[6] Vallowe, Ed F., *Biblical Mathematics: Keys to Scripture Numerics: The Significance of Scripture Numbers Revealed in the Word of God*. (Columbia, SC: Olive, 1998), P. 108. Print.

[7] http://www.urbandictionary.com/define.php?term=New%20York%20Minute. N.p., n.d. Web. 06 Feb. 2013.

[8] Vallowe, Ed F. *Biblical Mathematics: Keys to Scripture Numerics : The Significance of Scripture Numbers Revealed in the Word of God*. (Columbia, SC: Olive, 1998), P. 115. Print.

[9] "Pollyanna." *Wikipedia*. Wikimedia Foundation, 02 June 2013. Web. 06 Feb. 2013.

[10] "CHAPTER 22Â ." *Www.heavendwellers.com*. N.p., n.d. Web. 06 Feb. 2013.

[11] Park, Alice. "Worries over Hillary's Health." *Time Magazine* (2013): 16. Print.

[12] Vallowe, Ed F., *Biblical Mathematics: Keys to Scripture Numerics : The Significance of Scripture Numbers Revealed in the Word of God*. (Columbia, SC: Olive, 1998), P. 140. Print.

[13] Ibid. p. 74.

[14] *Welcome | Brilliant Perspectives*. N.p., n.d. Web. 06 Feb. 2013.

[15] "Little House Books." *Little House Books*. N.p., n.d. Web. 06 Feb. 2013.

[16] ""The Perfect Storm Is About To Hit--June, July, and August of 2006"" *"The Perfect Storm Is About To Hit--June, July, and August of 2006"* N.p., n.d. Web. 07 Feb. 2013.

[17] Vallowe, Ed F., *Biblical Mathematics: Keys to Scripture Numerics : The Significance of Scripture Numbers Revealed in the Word of God*. (Columbia, SC: Olive, 1998), P. 85. Print.

[18] Ibid., p. 151.

[19] Ibid., p. 144.

[20] "MTI Center Home Â» MTI Center." *MTI Center Home Â» MTI Center*. N.p., n.d. Web. 05 Feb. 2013.

[21] "Coral Snake on the Loose - Experts Forum at VenomousReptiles.org." *Coral Snake on the Loose - Experts Forum at VenomousReptiles.org*. N.p., n.d. Web. 05 Feb. 2013.

[22] "Arrest." *Dictionary.com*. Dictionary.com, n.d. Web. 05 Feb. 2013.

[23] *Evangelist Ed. F. Vallowe, Biblical Mathematics, Keys to Scripture Numerics, (Columbia, South Carolina, The Olive Press, 1998), P. 150.* N.p.: n.p., n.d. Print.

[24] "Oldsmobile 98." *Wikipedia*. Wikimedia Foundation, 02 June 2013. Web. 07 Feb. 2013.

[25] "Silver City, Idaho." *Wikipedia*. Wikimedia Foundation, 02 June 2013. Web. 07 Feb. 2013.

[26] Contributor, EHow. "How to Pray the A.C.T.S. Prayer." *EHow*. Demand Media, 15 Aug. 2009. Web. 07 Feb. 2013.

[27] "Staff and Wire Reports, "Death Toll Rises as Tornadoes Storm Their Way across State", Tulsa World, 4 May, 1999, Final Home Edition, Front Page." n.d.: n. pag. Print.

[28] *The Associated Press, "Tornado Touches down during Oklahoma City Rush Hour", Boise, Idaho, The Idaho Statesman, 5 May, 1999, P. 13A.* n.d.: n. pag. Print.

[29] Jason Collington, "Tornadoes Kill 36 in Midwest", The Associated Press, Boise, Idaho, The Idaho Statesman, 4 May, 1999, Front Page. N.d.: N. Pag. Print. n.d.: n. pag. Print.

[30] *Ron Jenkins, "Tornadoes Leave Lives, Homes in Ruins", The Associated Press, Boise, Idaho, The Idaho Statesman, 5 May, 1999, Front Page.* n.d.: n. pag. Print.

[31] *Jack Douglas, Jr. and Mike Lee, "Tornadoes Rip Open Oklahoma City's Wounds", Knight Ridder Newspapers, Boise, Idaho, The Idaho Statesman, 5 May, 1999, P. 4A.* n.d.: n. pag. Print.

[32] *Barbara Hoberock, Rod Walton, Brian Ford, Omer Gillham, David Fallis, Tim Hoover and Patti Weaver, "Oklahomans Begin to Pick up the Pieces of Nature's Wrath", World Staff Writers, Tulsa, Oklahoma, Tulsa World, 5 May, 1999, Final Home Edition, Front Page. n.d.: n. pag. Print.*

[33] *Alan Levin and Scott Bowles, "Oklahomans Will Rebuild – Houses, Businesses, Towns in Ruins", USA Today, Boise, Idaho, The Idaho Statesman, 6 May, 1999, Front Page. n.d.: n. pag. Print.*

[34] Keesee, Ruby, Bible Studies for Women: The Gift of the Word of Knowledge (Caldwell, Idaho, 1990), PP. 1-4.

Keesee, Ruby, Bible Studies for Women: The Gift of the Word of Wisdom (Caldwell, Idaho, 1990), PP. 1-2.

[35] Keesee, Ruby, Bible Studies for Women: The Gift of Discerning of Spirits, (Caldwell, Idaho, 1990), PP. 1-4.

Sheila F. Eismann

www.ingramcontent.com/pod-product-compliance
Lightning Source LLC
Chambersburg PA
CBHW070556100426
42744CB00006B/300